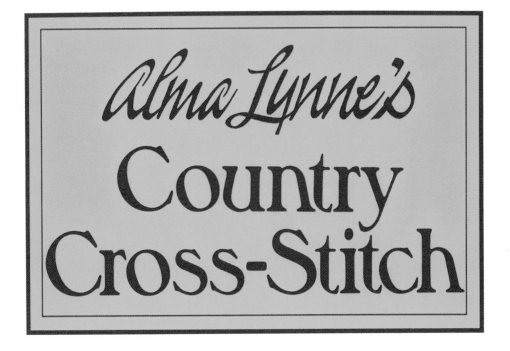

Alma Lynne's
Country Cross-Stitch

Oxmoor House®

Library of Congress Catalog Number: 90-62048
ISBN: 0-8487-1014-2
Manufactured in the United States of America
First Printing 1990

Executive Editor: Nancy Janice Fitzpatrick
Production Manager: Jerry Higdon
Associate Production Manager: Rick Litton
Art Director: Bob Nance
Copy Chief: Mary Jean Haddin

Alma Lynne's Country Cross-Stitch

Editor: Brenda Waldron Kolb
Assistant Editors: Laurie Anne Pate, Kim Eidson Crane
Assistant Copy Editor: Susan Smith Cheatham
Production Assistant: Theresa L. Beste
Designer: Melissa Jones Clark
Computer Artist: Karen L. Tindall
Artist: Eleanor Cameron
Photostylist: Katie Stoddard
Photographers: John O'Hagan, Art Meripol

To find out how you can order *Cooking Light* magazine, write to *Cooking Light*®, P.O. Box C-549, Birmingham, AL 35283

Contents

Country Critters

Country Wisdom

Country Children

Country Christmas

Country Kitchen

All-American Country

Welcome

Thank you, fellow stitcher, for giving my book a place in your cross-stitch library. For me, it is the fruit of many pleasurable hours spent with my graph paper and pen. At my drafting table or at my kitchen table, in my studio or in restaurants, I drew and redrew my cross-stitch designs, which eventually filled over 100 pamphlets. In this, my first hardcover book, I've gathered some of the best. Creating these designs was truly a labor of love, and I am proud to see them in this beautiful volume.

The designs are near and dear to my heart, for they reflect a subject, a style, that I'm extremely fond of. A decidedly country feeling distinguishes each of them, from the old-time proverbs and Americana motifs to the lop-eared bunnies and sweet-faced teddy bears. If you're looking for a little country flavor, a little country flair, you'll find it here, from the first page to the last.

So, settle back in your favorite stitching chair (we all have one—it's the chair with the permanent impression of our backside). Now you're ready to relax and enjoy many happy hours of stitching. Best of all, at the end of those pleasant hours, you will have created country cross-stitch treasures for family and friends to last a lifetime.

I proudly dedicate this book to
my life's partner and best friend,
Scoot,
and to my greatest joys, sons
Clay and Seth.
You all are my life!

Yours in cross-stitch,

Alma Lynne

Country Critters

I've always had a warm and fuzzy feeling for teddy bears. I've collected them for as long as I can remember. In fact, I've sometimes had to rearrange or even eliminate pieces of furniture in my home in order to make room for them.

Other longtime favorites are country cats. To me, these feline fanciers of sunny window-sills and rugs by the hearth symbolize domestic comfort and quiet contentment.

Of late, lop-eared bunnies have captured my heart. In creating these imaginary friends, I have tried to show their playful innocence and to bring them to life in the lines of their expressions and dress.

I hope that you enjoy stitching these furry and fanciful country critters as much as I've enjoyed designing them.

Bunny Bear

Sample in photograph was stitched on mushroom 25-count Lugana over 2 threads. Design area is 4⅜″ x 8⅜″. Fabric was cut 11″ x 15″.

FABRICS	DESIGN AREAS
11-count	4⅞″ x 9½″
14-count	3⅞″ x 7⅜″
18-count	3″ x 5¾″
22-count	2½″ x 4¾″

104
54

DMC Colors
(used for sample)

Step 1: Cross-stitch (2 strands)

C	⌐		White
•	◢	310	Black
+	◿	353	Peach
✳	◿	415	Pearl Gray
＼	◺	754	Peach-lt.
V	◿	762	Pearl Gray-vy. lt.
X	◿	838	Beige Brown-vy. dk.
6	◢	839	Beige Brown-dk.
S	◿	840	Beige Brown-med.
I	◿	841	Beige Brown-lt.
╱	◿	842	Beige Brown-vy. lt.
O	◢	948	Peach-vy. lt.

Step 2: Half-cross (2 strands)

╱	◿	646	Beaver Gray-dk.

Step 3: Backstitch (1 strand)

	3371 Black Brown

Step 4: Bow (6 strands)

White (Thread floss in and out at marked points and tie in bow.)

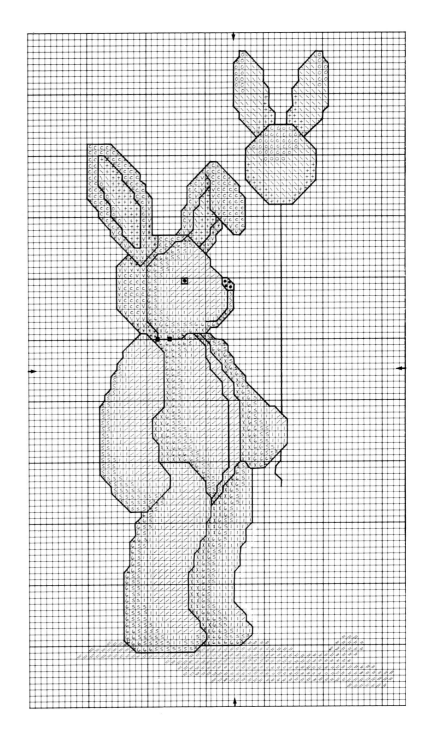

Country Cats

SAMPLE

Sample in photograph was stitched on ivory 14-count Aida over 1 thread. Design area is 3¾" x 5⅜". Fabric was cut 10" x 12".

FABRICS	DESIGN AREAS
11-count	4¾" x 6⅞"
18-count	2⅞" x 4⅛"
22-count	2⅜" x 3⅜"

75
52

DMC Colors (used for sample)

Step 1: Cross-stitch (2 strands)

•			White
C		221	Shell Pink-vy. dk.
^		223	Shell Pink-med.
\		224	Shell Pink-lt.
X		312	Navy Blue-lt.
V		322	Navy Blue-vy. lt.
/		334	Baby Blue-med.
−		775	Baby Blue-vy. lt.
3		902	Garnet-vy. dk.
O		3325	Baby Blue-lt.

Step 2: Backstitch (1 strand)

	311	Navy Blue-med. (lettering)
	3371	Black Brown (all else)

Step 3: Long Loose Stitch (1 strand)

	3371	Black Brown

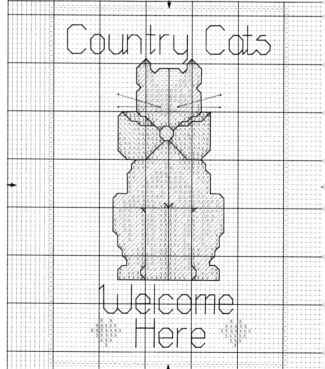

Bertha Ann Bunnyhatch

MATERIALS

Completed cross-stitch on cream/tan 28-count
   Chalet; matching thread
1¼ yards (45"-wide) green print; matching thread
⅝ yard (45"-wide) coral print
4 yards (⅛"-wide) cream satin ribbon
4 yards (⅛"-wide) coral satin ribbon
4 yards (⅛"-wide) green satin ribbon
4 yards (1/16"-wide) light coral satin ribbon
Dressmakers' pen
Stuffing

INSTRUCTIONS

All seam allowances are ¼".

1. With design centered, trim Chalet to 6½" x 11½". From green print, cut 4 (45" x 9") strips for ruffle; also cut 2 (15" x 2¼") strips and 2

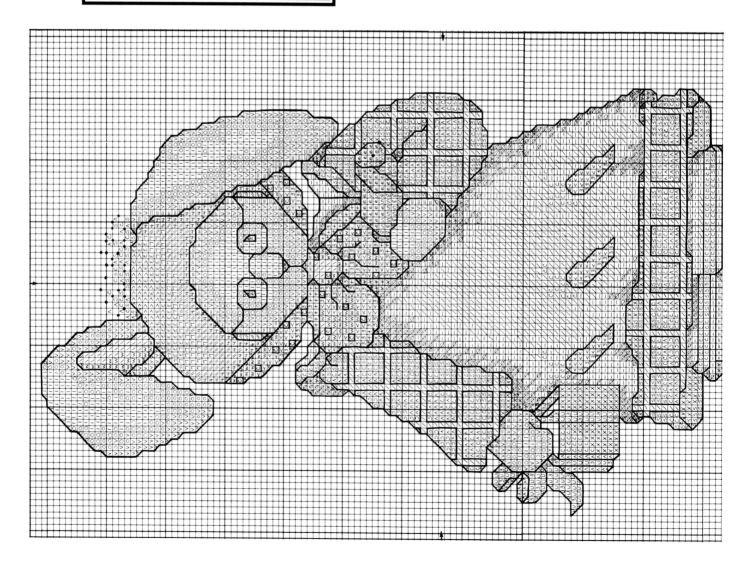

(6½" x 2¼") strips for border. From coral print, cut 1 (15½" x 20½") piece for pillow back; also cut 2 (15½" x 3¼") strips and 2 (15" x 3¼") strips for border.

2. To make pillow front: Use dressmakers' pen to mark center of 1 long edge of each green border strip and center of each edge of design piece. With right sides facing, raw edges aligned, and center marks matching, sew short green strips to top and bottom of design piece and then long green strips to sides. Mark and sew coral border strips to green border strips in same manner, except first sew short strips to sides and then long strips to top and bottom.

3. With right sides facing and raw edges aligned, stitch ends of 4 (45" x 9") green strips together to make 1 (178½" x 9") strip. With right sides facing and raw edges aligned, fold the strip in half lengthwise to measure 4½" wide; stitch ends. Turn and press. Run gathering threads along raw edges through both layers. Mark ruffle at 38", 89", and 127". Beginning at bottom left-hand corner, pin ruffle to right side of pillow front, aligning raw edges and placing marks at corners. Gather ruffle to fit. Stitch along stitching line of piping, through all layers.

4. Place pillow back over front, with right sides facing, raw edges aligned, and ruffle toward center. Stitch, leaving an opening on 1 side. Turn. Stuff firmly. Slipstitch opening closed.

5. Cut each ribbon into 4 equal lengths. Separate ribbons into 4 sets, with each set containing 1 ribbon of each color. Holding all ribbons as 1, tie 1 set of ribbons into a bow and tack to 1 outside corner of green border. Repeat to tack 3 more bows to 3 remaining corners of green border.

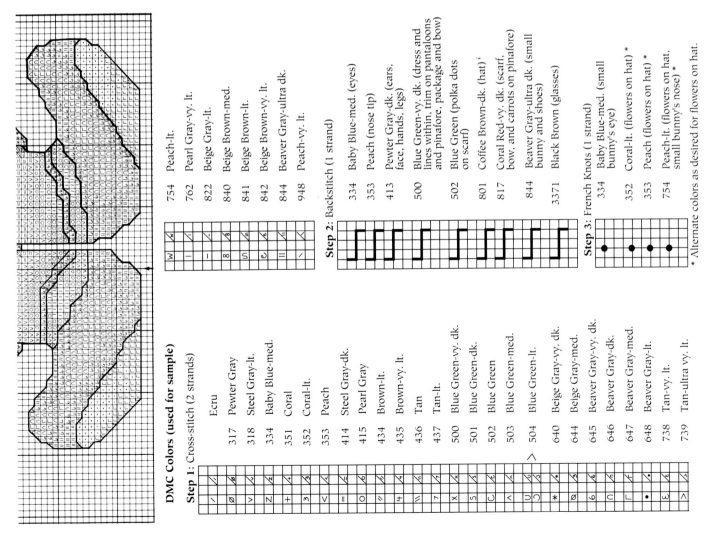

13

Everybunny's Welcome

73
100

DMC Colors (used for sample)

Step 1: Cross-stitch (2 strands)

•	⁄		White
Z	⁄	223	Shell Pink-med.
C	⁄	224	Shell Pink-lt.
∧	⁄	318	Steel Gray-lt.
S	⁄	414	Steel Gray-dk.
O	⁄	415	Pearl Gray
3	⁄	501	Blue Green-dk.
⁄⁄	⁄	502	Blue Green
⊠	⁄	503	Blue Green-med.
Γ	⁄	504	Blue Green-lt.
⁄	⁄	762	Pearl Gray-vy. lt.

*	⁄	839	Beige Brown-dk.
Ø	⁄	840	Beige Brown-med.
L	⁄	841	Beige Brown-lt.
I	⁄	842	Beige Brown-vy. lt.
X	⁄	930	Antique Blue-dk.
V	⁄	931	Antique Blue-med.
\	⁄	932	Antique Blue-lt.

Step 2: Backstitch (1 strand)

L		310	Black

Step 3: French Knots (1 strand)

●		310	Black

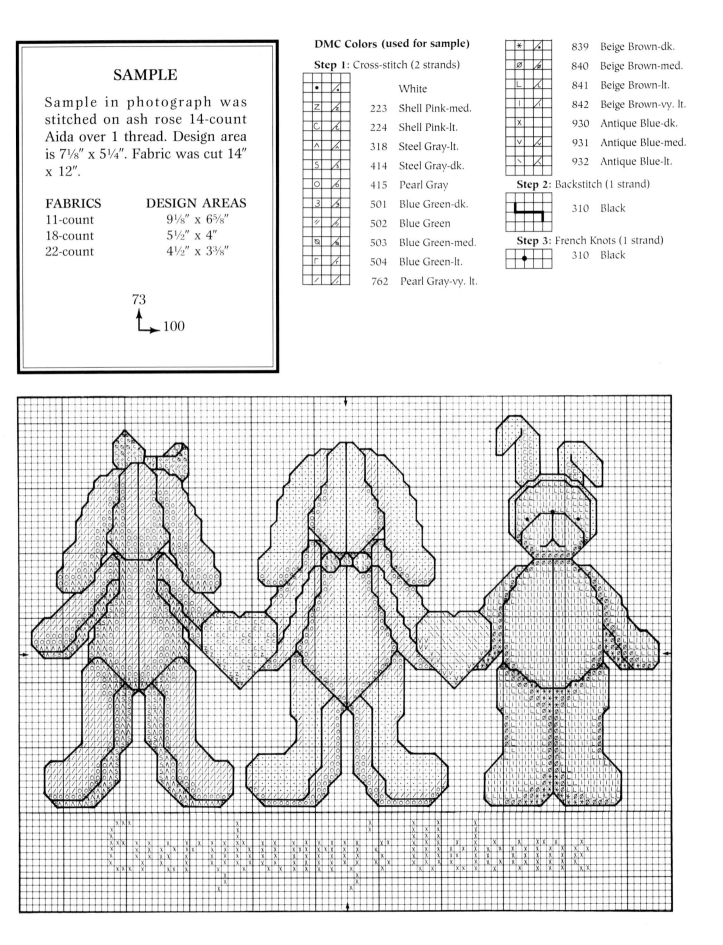

15

Country Miniatures

SAMPLES

Samples in photograph were stitched on mushroom 25-count Lugana over 2 threads. Design areas are: kitty, 1¾" x 2¾"; teddy, 1½" x 2¾"; and bunny, 1⅝" x 3¼". Fabric was cut 8" x 10" for each.

Miniature dressing screens (Stock No. 14235 for pink screen, Stock No. 14239 for blue screen) were supplied by The Spinning Wheel, 48 East Madison Avenue, Milton, WI 53563.

Kitty

FABRICS	DESIGN AREAS	34
11-count	2" x 3⅛"	↑ 22
14-count	1⅝" x 2⅜"	
18-count	1¼" x 1⅞"	
22-count	1" x 1½"	

Teddy

FABRICS	DESIGN AREAS	34
11-count	1¾" x 3⅛"	↑ 19
14-count	1⅜" x 2⅜"	
18-count	1" x 1⅞"	
22-count	⅞" x 1½"	

Bunny

FABRICS	DESIGN AREAS	40
11-count	1⅞" x 3⅝"	↑ 20
14-count	1⅜" x 2⅞"	
18-count	1⅛" x 2¼"	
22-count	⅞" x 1⅞"	

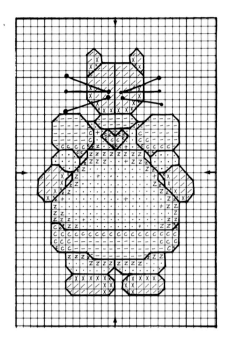

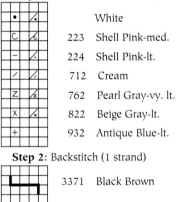

DMC Colors
(used for sample)

Step 1: Cross-stitch (2 strands)

•	∕	White
C	∠	223 Shell Pink-med.
−	∕	224 Shell Pink-lt.
∕	∕	712 Cream
Z	∠	762 Pearl Gray-vy. lt.
X	∕	822 Beige Gray-lt.
+		932 Antique Blue-lt.

Step 2: Backstitch (1 strand)

⌐	3371 Black Brown

Step 3: Long Loose Stitch (1 strand)

	3371 Black Brown

DMC Colors
(used for sample)

Step 1: Cross-stitch (2 strands)

C	∠	221 Shell Pink-vy. dk.
X	∕	437 Tan-lt.
O	∕	738 Tan-vy. lt.
∕	∕	739 Tan-ultra vy. lt.
Z	∠	924 Slate Green-vy. dk.
\	∕	926 Slate Green
7	∕	927 Slate Green-med.

Step 2: Backstitch (1 strand)

⌐	3371 Black Brown

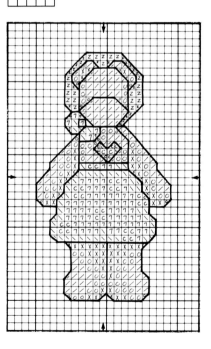

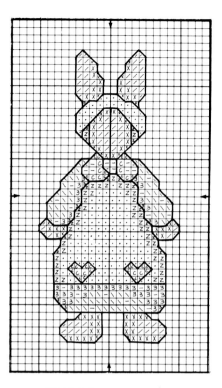

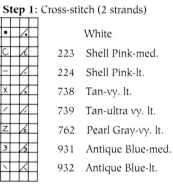

DMC Colors
(used for sample)

Step 1: Cross-stitch (2 strands)

•	∕	White
C	∠	223 Shell Pink-med.
−	∕	224 Shell Pink-lt.
X	∕	738 Tan-vy. lt.
∕	∕	739 Tan-ultra vy. lt.
Z	∠	762 Pearl Gray-vy. lt.
3	∕	931 Antique Blue-med.
		932 Antique Blue-lt.

Step 2: Backstitch (1 strand)

⌐	3371 Black Brown

Golden Bear

SAMPLE	FABRICS	DESIGN AREAS	
Sample in photograph was stitched on celadon 14-count Aida over 2 threads. Design area is 9¾" x 10⅜". Fabric was cut 16" x 17".	11-count	6⅛" x 6⅝"	
	14-count	4¾" x 5¼"	73
	18-count	3¾" x 4"	67
	22-count	3" x 3⅜"	

DMC Colors (used for sample)

Step 1: Cross-stitch (3 strands)

•	⁄	Ecru
O	6	White
■	⁄	310 Black
◣	⁄	433 Brown-med.
✳	⁄	434 Brown-lt.
X	⁄	435 Brown-vy. lt.
□	⁄	436 Tan
∧	⁄	437 Tan-lt.

Z	⁄	561 Jade-vy. dk.
H	⁄	562 Jade-med.
⁄	⁄	563 Jade-lt.
+	⁄	738 Tan-vy. lt.
\	⁄	739 Tan-ultra vy. lt.
●	⁄	801 Coffee Brown-dk.
−	⁄	815 Garnet-med.
I	⁄	902 Garnet-vy. dk.
C	⁄	924 Slate Green-vy. dk.
◥	⁄	926 Slate Green

N	⁄	927 Slate Green-med.
3	⁄	928 Slate Green-lt.

Step 2: Half-cross (3 strands)

U	⁄	838 Beige Brown-vy. dk.

Step 3: Backstitch (1 strand)

L	310 Black

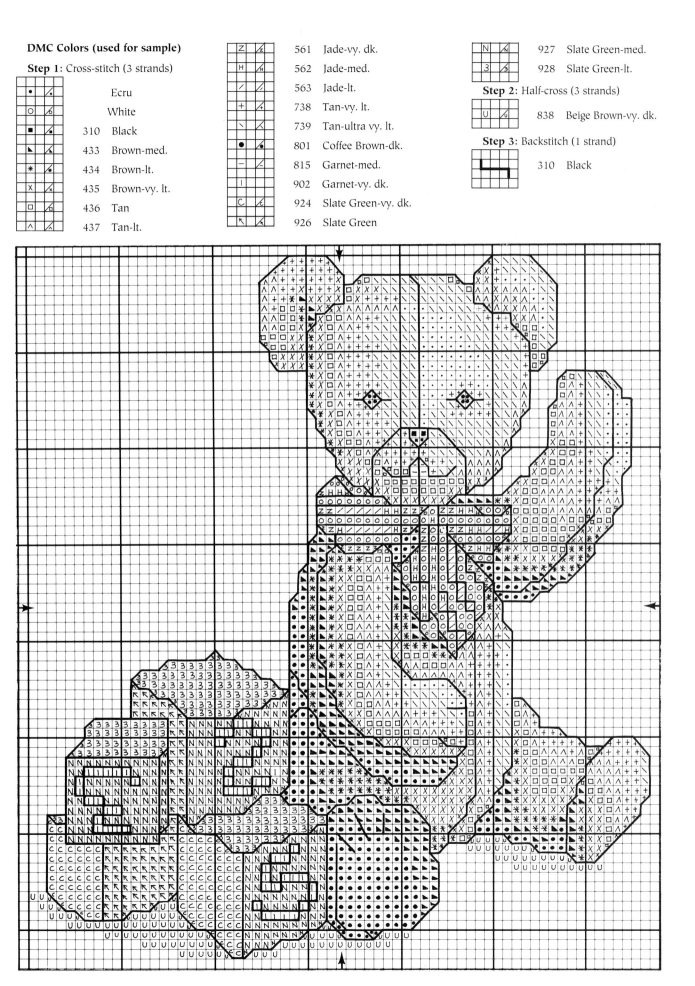

Somebunny's Friend

SAMPLE

Sample in photograph was stitched on bluebell 30-count Shannon over 2 threads. Design area is 8″ x 8¼″. Fabric was cut 14″ x 15″.

FABRICS	DESIGN AREAS
11-count	10⅞″ x 11⅛″
14-count	8⅝″ x 8¾″
18-count	6⅝″ x 6⅞″
22-count	5½″ x 5⅝″

123
↑
└→ 120

MATERIALS

Completed cross-stitch on bluebell 30-count Shannon; matching thread
⅜ yard (45″-wide) yellow fabric; matching thread
⅝ yard (45″-wide) blue print; matching thread
1⅜ yards of small cording
Dressmakers' pen
Stuffing

INSTRUCTIONS

All seam allowances are ¼″.

1. With design centered, trim Shannon to 11½″ x 11½″ for pillow front. From yellow fabric, cut 1 (11½″) square for pillow back and 4 (27½″ x 2½″) strips for ruffle. From blue print, cut 4 (27½″ x 5½″) strips for ruffle; also cut 1″-wide bias strips, piecing as needed to equal 48″. With bias strip and cording, make 48″ of corded piping.

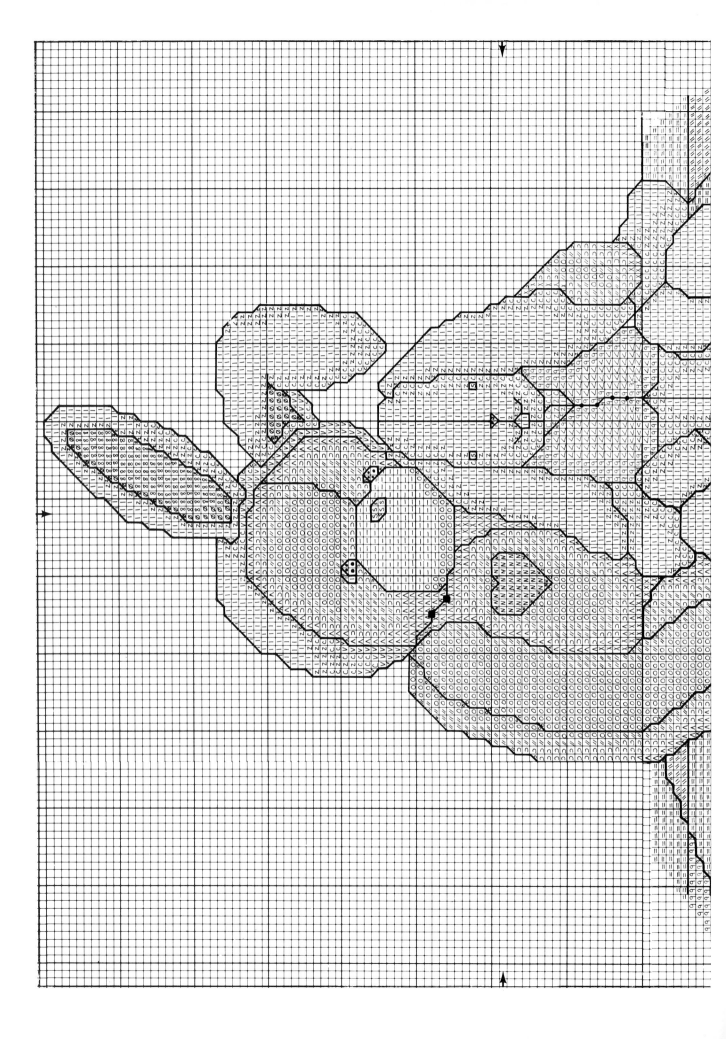

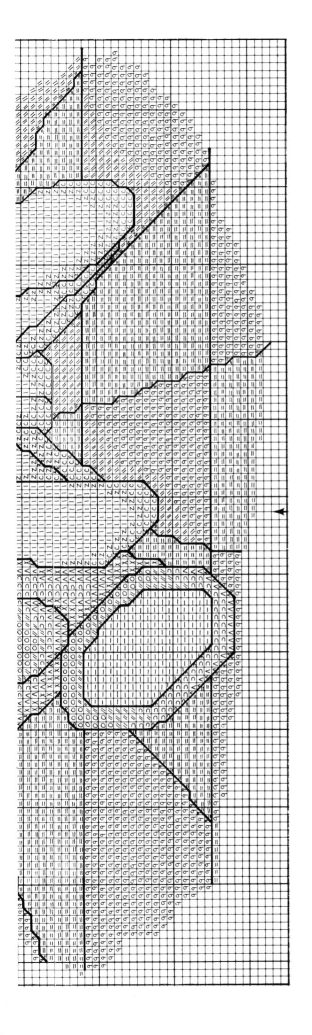

2. With right sides facing and raw edges aligned, baste piping around all edges of pillow front.

3. With right sides facing and raw edges aligned, stitch ends of yellow strips together to make 1 (108½″ x 2½″) strip. In same manner, stitch ends of blue print strips together to make 1 (108½″ x 5½″) strip. Press seams open. With right sides facing, raw edges aligned, and seams matching, stitch yellow strip to blue print strip along 1 long edge to make 1 (108½″ x 7½″) strip.

4. With right sides facing and raw edges aligned, fold strip in half lengthwise to measure 3¾″ wide; stitch ends. Turn and press. Run gathering threads along raw edges through both layers. Divide ruffle into 4ths and mark. With yellow/blue side of ruffle facing right side of pillow front, pin ruffle to pillow front, aligning raw edges and placing marks at corners. Gather to fit. Stitch along stitching line for piping, through all layers.

5. Place pillow back over front, with right sides facing, raw edges aligned, and piping and ruffle toward center. Stitch, leaving opening on 1 side. Trim corners and turn. Stuff firmly. Slipstitch opening closed.

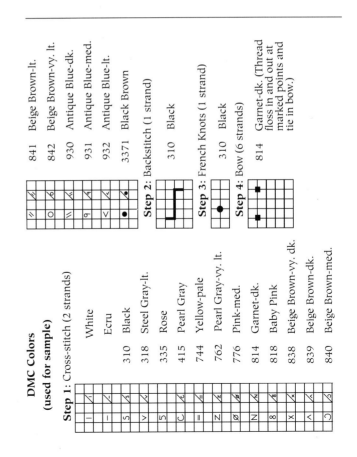

Alphabet Bunny

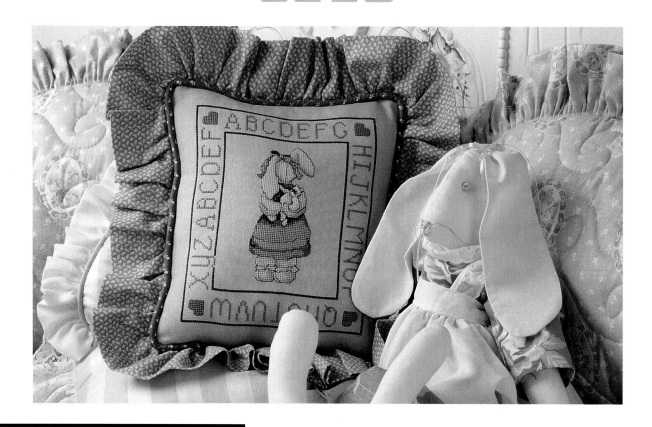

SAMPLE

Sample in photograph was stitched on tan 28-count Jubilee over 2 threads. Design area is 7¼″ x 8¾″. Fabric was cut 14″ x 15″.

FABRICS	DESIGN AREAS
11-count	9⅛″ x 11⅛″
14-count	7¼″ x 8¾″
18-count	5⅝″ x 6¾″
22-count	4⅝″ x 5½″

122
↑
└→ 101

MATERIALS

Completed cross-stitch on ivory 28-count Jubilee; matching thread
½ yard (45″-wide) pink-and-white print; matching thread
¼ yard (45″-wide) blue-and-white print; matching thread
1⅜ yards of medium cording
Dressmakers' pen
Stuffing

INSTRUCTIONS

All seam allowances are ¼″.

1. With design centered, trim Jubilee to 9¾″ x 11¼″. From pink-and-white print, cut 1 (9¾″ x 11¼″) piece for pillow back and 3 (33½″ x 5½″) strips for ruffle. From blue-and-white print, cut

1½"-wide bias strips, piecing as needed to equal 46". With bias strip and cording, make 46" of corded piping.

2. With right sides facing and raw edges aligned, pin piping around all edges of pillow front. Baste piping in place.

3. To make ruffle: With right sides facing and raw edges aligned, stitch ends of 3 pink-and-white strips together to make 1 (100½" x 5½") strip. With right sides facing and raw edges aligned, fold strip in half lengthwise to measure

2¾" wide; stitch ends. Turn and press. Run gathering threads along raw edges through both layers. Divide ruffle into 4ths and mark. Pin ruffle to right side of pillow front, aligning raw edges and placing marks at corners. Gather ruffle to fit. Stitch along stitching line for piping, through all layers.

4. Place pillow back over front, with right sides facing, raw edges aligned, and piping and ruffle toward center. Stitch, leaving an opening on 1 side. Trim corners and turn. Stuff firmly. Slip-stitch opening closed.

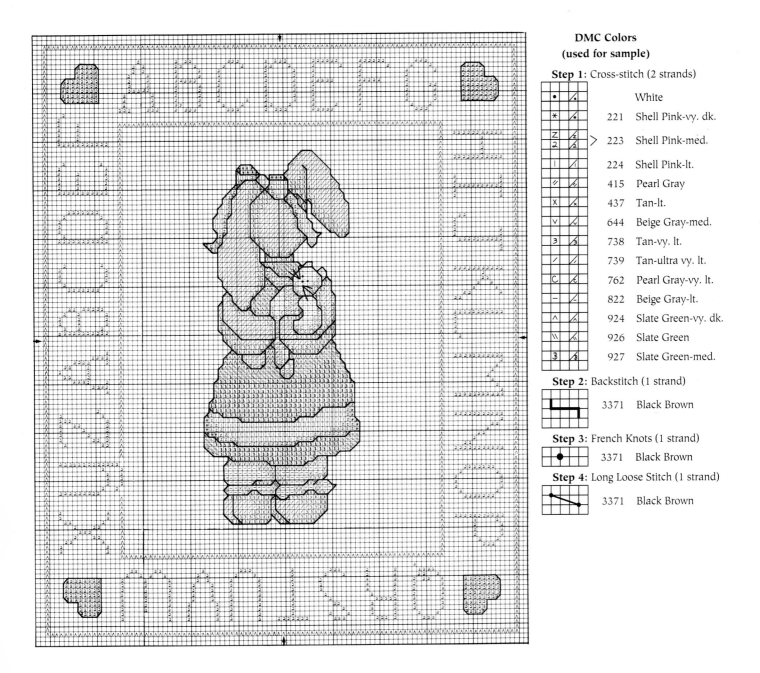

DMC Colors
(used for sample)

Step 1: Cross-stitch (2 strands)

•	⁄		White
*	⁄	221	Shell Pink-vy. dk.
Z / 2	⁄	223	Shell Pink-med.
I	⁄	224	Shell Pink-lt.
"	⁄	415	Pearl Gray
X	⁄	437	Tan-lt.
V	⁄	644	Beige Gray-med.
3	⁄	738	Tan-vy. lt.
/	⁄	739	Tan-ultra vy. lt.
C	⁄	762	Pearl Gray-vy. lt.
–	⁄	822	Beige Gray-lt.
^	⁄	924	Slate Green-vy. dk.
\\	⁄	926	Slate Green
3	⁄	927	Slate Green-med.

Step 2: Backstitch (1 strand)

⌐	3371	Black Brown

Step 3: French Knots (1 strand)

•	3371	Black Brown

Step 4: Long Loose Stitch (1 strand)

╲	3371	Black Brown

Country Wisdom

Memories of childhood are special blessings. Impressions sink deep then, and words from beloved grown-ups may stay with us all our lives.

Mom Berta, my grand-mother, steered our family with a firm but gentle hand. As one of her thirteen grandchildren, I competed for, and occasionally seemed to win, her favor. Though I didn't realize it at the time, the true spoils of my victories were the lessons on life that she imparted to me then and that I often find myself repeating now.

In fact, I've memorialized in cross-stitch designs some of Mom Berta's words of wisdom. I think she would be proud (and maybe a little surprised!) to see that her granddaughter not only remembers, but lives by and shares, her words.

Best Friends

SAMPLE

Sample in photograph was stitched on ivory 28-count Jubilee over 2 threads. Design area is 7½″ x 9¼″. Fabric was cut 14″ x 16″.

FABRICS	DESIGN AREAS
11-count	9½″ x 11⅞″
14-count	7½″ x 9¼″
18-count	5⅞″ x 7¼″
22-count	4¾″ x 5⅞″

130
↑
└→105

Happiness

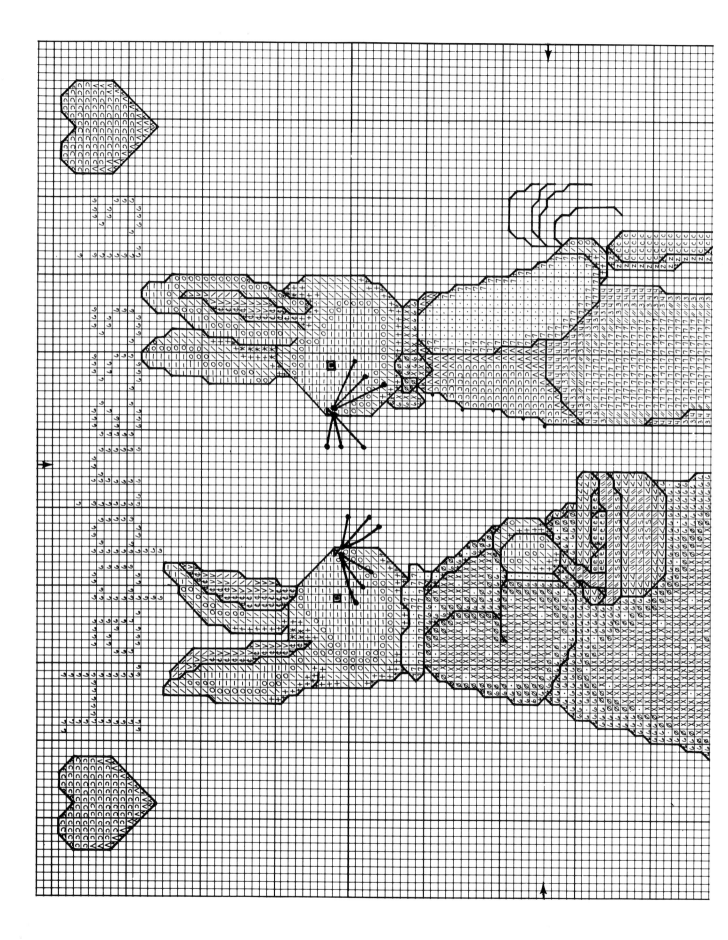

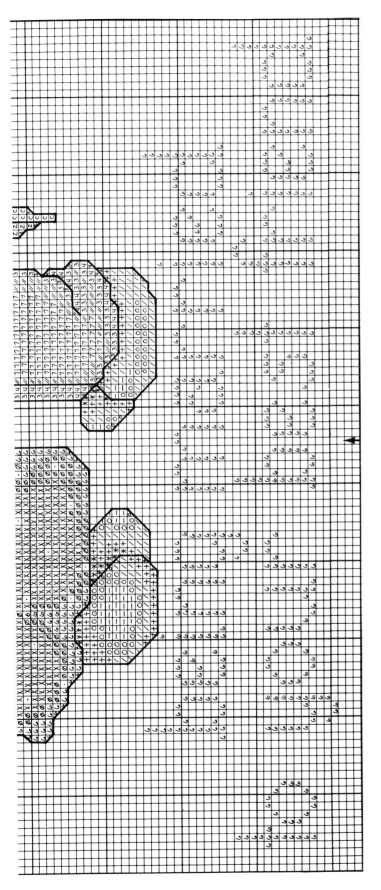

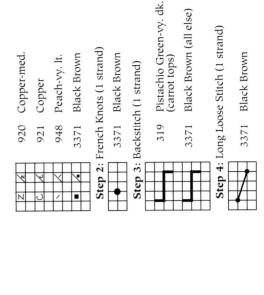

Z	920	Copper-med.
C	921	Copper
⟋	948	Peach-vy. lt.
■	3371	Black Brown

Step 2: French Knots (1 strand)

●	3371	Black Brown

Step 3: Backstitch (1 strand)

319 | Pistachio Green-vy. dk. (carrot tops)

3371 | Black Brown (all else)

Step 4: Long Loose Stitch (1 strand)

3371 | Black Brown

<		437	Tan-lt.
∖		738	Tan-vy. lt.
S		739	Tan-ultra vy. lt.
∨		754	Peach-lt.
7		762	Pearl Gray-vy. lt.
*		838	Beige Brown-vy. dk.
+		839	Beige Brown-dk.
∕		840	Beige Brown-med.
O		841	Beige Brown-lt.
−		842	Beige Brown-vy. lt.

DMC Colors
(used for sample)

Step 1: Cross-stitch (2 strands)

•			White
℮			Ecru
3		318	Steel Gray-lt.
6		319	Pistachio Green-vy. dk.
X		320	Pistachio Green-med.
C		353	Peach
<		355	Terra Cotta-dk.
C		356	Terra Cotta-med.
Ø		367	Pistachio Green-dk.
+		414	Steel Gray-dk.
∕		415	Pearl Gray

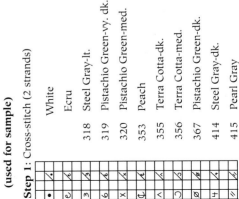

31

Gift of Love

SAMPLE

Sample in photograph was stitched on ivory 14-count Aida over 1 thread. Design area is 3⅞" x 4⅞". Fabric was cut 11" x 12".

FABRICS	DESIGN AREAS
11-count	5" x 6¼"
18-count	3" x 3⅞"
22-count	2½" x 3⅛"

69
→ 55

DMC Colors (used for sample)
Step 1: Cross-stitch (2 strands)

		DMC	Color
●	╱	223	Shell Pink-med.
╲	╱	224	Shell Pink-lt.
X	╱	434	Brown-lt.
V	╱	435	Brown-vy. lt.
C	╱	436	Tan
╱	╱	437	Tan-lt.
Z	╱	502	Blue Green
∧	╱	503	Blue Green-med.
•	╱	738	Tan-vy. lt.

Step 2: French Knots (1 strand)

	DMC	Color
●	223	Shell Pink-med.
■	224	Shell Pink-lt.

Step 3: Backstitch (1 strand)

	DMC	Color
	501	Blue Green-dk. (lettering, flower stems)
	3371	Black Brown (all else)

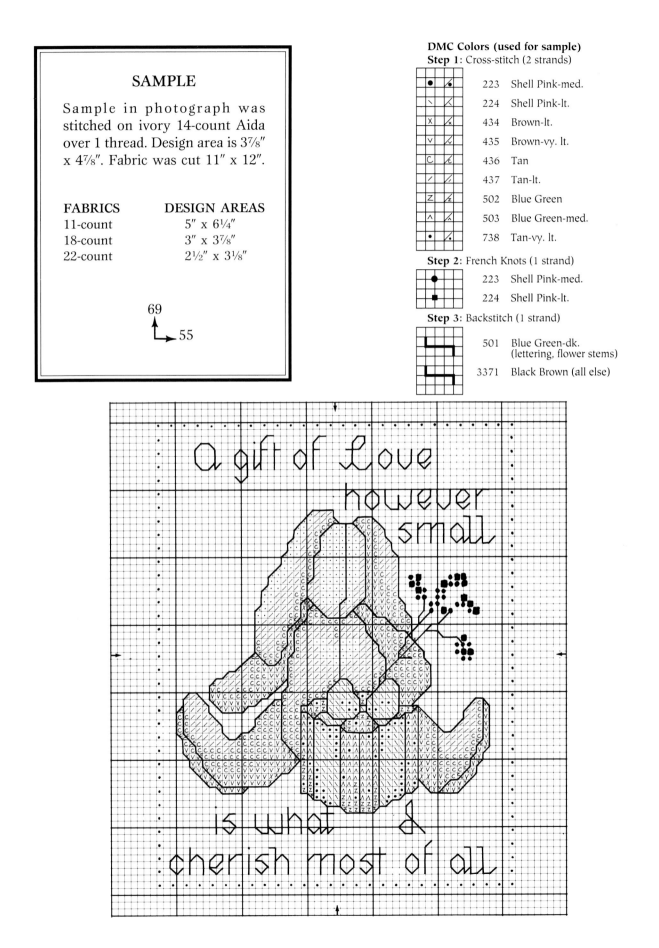

For Mom

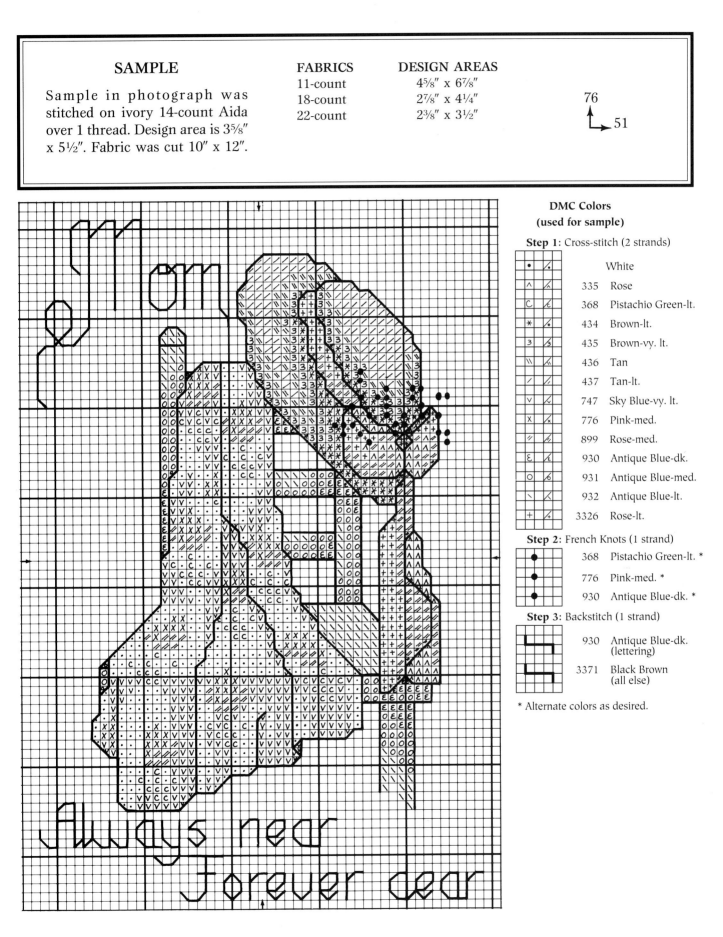

SAMPLE

Sample in photograph was stitched on ivory 14-count Aida over 1 thread. Design area is 3⅝" x 5½". Fabric was cut 10" x 12".

FABRICS
11-count
18-count
22-count

DESIGN AREAS
4⅝" x 6⅞"
2⅞" x 4¼"
2⅜" x 3½"

76
↑
└→ 51

DMC Colors
(used for sample)

Step 1: Cross-stitch (2 strands)

•	⁄.		White
∧	⁄⁄	335	Rose
C	⁄⁄	368	Pistachio Green-lt.
*	⁄⁄	434	Brown-lt.
3	⁄⁄	435	Brown-vy. lt.
\\	⁄⁄	436	Tan
⁄	⁄⁄	437	Tan-lt.
V	⁄⁄	747	Sky Blue-vy. lt.
X	⁄⁄	776	Pink-med.
⁄⁄	⁄⁄	899	Rose-med.
Ɛ	⁄⁄	930	Antique Blue-dk.
O	⁄⁄	931	Antique Blue-med.
\	⁄⁄	932	Antique Blue-lt.
+	⁄⁄	3326	Rose-lt.

Step 2: French Knots (1 strand)

•	368 Pistachio Green-lt. *
•	776 Pink-med. *
•	930 Antique Blue-dk. *

Step 3: Backstitch (1 strand)

	930 Antique Blue-dk. (lettering)
	3371 Black Brown (all else)

* Alternate colors as desired.

35

For Dad

DMC Colors (used for sample)

Step 1: Cross-stitch (2 strands)

•	⁄		White
V	⁄		Ecru
Z	⁄	317	Pewter Gray
+	⁄	498	Christmas Red-dk.
Ƶ	⁄	645	Beaver Gray-vy. dk.
∧	⁄	762	Pearl Gray-vy. lt.
O	6	815	Garnet-med.
\	⁄	823	Navy Blue-dk.
S	3	902	Garnet-vy. dk.
C	⁄	3022	Brown Gray-med.
X	⁄	3023	Brown Gray-lt.

Step 2: Backstitch (1 strand)

	645	Beaver Gray-vy. dk. (stripes on wallpaper)
	902	Garnet-vy. dk. (lettering)
	3371	Black Brown (all else)

Home Sewn

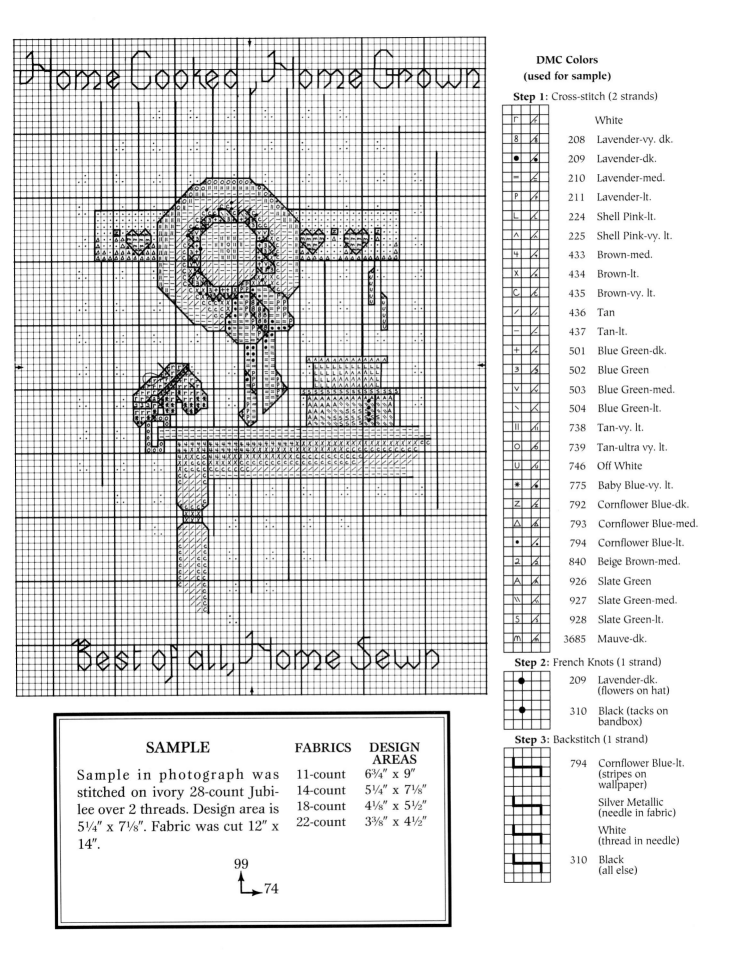

DMC Colors
(used for sample)

Step 1: Cross-stitch (2 strands)

⌐	⌐		White
8	8	208	Lavender-vy. dk.
●	●	209	Lavender-dk.
=	=	210	Lavender-med.
P	P	211	Lavender-lt.
L	L	224	Shell Pink-lt.
∧	∧	225	Shell Pink-vy. lt.
4	4	433	Brown-med.
X	X	434	Brown-lt.
C	C	435	Brown-vy. lt.
/	/	436	Tan
−	−	437	Tan-lt.
+	+	501	Blue Green-dk.
3	3	502	Blue Green
V	V	503	Blue Green-med.
\	\	504	Blue Green-lt.
‖	‖	738	Tan-vy. lt.
O	O	739	Tan-ultra vy. lt.
U	U	746	Off White
*	*	775	Baby Blue-vy. lt.
Z	Z	792	Cornflower Blue-dk.
△	△	793	Cornflower Blue-med.
•	•	794	Cornflower Blue-lt.
2	2	840	Beige Brown-med.
A	A	926	Slate Green
⧵	⧵	927	Slate Green-med.
S	S	928	Slate Green-lt.
m	m	3685	Mauve-dk.

Step 2: French Knots (1 strand)

●	209	Lavender-dk. (flowers on hat)
●	310	Black (tacks on bandbox)

Step 3: Backstitch (1 strand)

	794	Cornflower Blue-lt. (stripes on wallpaper)
		Silver Metallic (needle in fabric)
		White (thread in needle)
	310	Black (all else)

SAMPLE	FABRICS	DESIGN AREAS
Sample in photograph was stitched on ivory 28-count Jubilee over 2 threads. Design area is 5¼″ x 7⅛″. Fabric was cut 12″ x 14″.	11-count	6¾″ x 9″
	14-count	5¼″ x 7⅛″
	18-count	4⅛″ x 5½″
	22-count	3⅜″ x 4½″

99
↑→74

Rain or Shine

SAMPLES

Samples in photograph were stitched on ivory 14-count Aida over 1 thread. Design areas are 3⅝″ x 4½″ for Raindrops, 3¾″ x 4⅝″ for Sunshine. Fabric was cut 10″ x 11″ for each.

Raindrops

FABRICS	DESIGN AREAS
11-count	4⅝″ x 5⅝″
18-count	2⅞″ x 3½″
22-count	2⅜″ x 2⅞″

62
↑
└→51

Sunshine

FABRICS	DESIGN AREAS
11-count	4¾″ x 5¾″
18-count	2⅞″ x 3½″
22-count	2⅜″ x 2⅞″

64
↑
└→52

Raindrops

DMC Colors
(used for sample)

Step 1: Cross-stitch (2 strands)

X	⊿	312 Navy Blue-lt.
∧	⊿	322 Navy Blue-vy. lt.
–	⟋	334 Baby Blue-med.
8	⊿	353 Peach
3	⊿	356 Terra Cotta-med.
″	⊿	434 Brown-lt.
L	⊿	435 Brown-vy. lt.
V	⊿	436 Tan
⟋	⊿	437 Tan-lt.
I	⟋	501 Blue Green-dk.

C	⊿	502 Blue Green
O	⊿	754 Peach-lt.
7	⟋	758 Terra Cotta-lt.
+	⟋	948 Peach-vy. lt.
•	⟋	3325 Baby Blue-lt.

Step 2: French Knots (1 strand)

●	3371 Black Brown

Step 3: Backstitch (1 strand)

902 Garnet-vy. dk. (lettering)
3325 Baby Blue-lt. (raindrops)
3371 Black Brown (all else)

Sunshine

DMC Colors
(used for sample)

Step 1: Cross-stitch (2 strands)

\\	350	Coral-med.
I	351	Coral
•	352	Coral-lt.
*	353	Peach
4	435	Brown-vy. lt.
v	436	Tan
-	437	Tan-lt.
Z	518	Wedgewood-lt.
+	519	Sky Blue

X	738	Tan-vy. lt.
\	739	Tan-ultra vy. lt.
/	754	Peach-lt.
O	948	Peach-vy. lt.

Step 2: Half-cross (2 strands)

//	738	Tan-vy. lt.

Step 3: Backstitch (1 strand)

	517	Wedgewood-dk. (lettering)
	3371	Black Brown (all else)

Friendship

SAMPLE

Sample in photograph was stitched on pewter 25-count Lugana over 2 threads. Design area is 6½" x 5¾". Fabric was cut 13" x 12".

FABRICS	DESIGN AREAS
11-count	7⅜" x 6½"
14-count	5¾" x 5⅛"
18-count	4½" x 4"
22-count	3⅝" x 3¼"

72 ← → 81

MATERIALS

Completed cross-stitch on pewter 25-count Lugana; matching thread
⅜ yard (45"-wide) red pindot; matching thread
1 yard (½"-wide) purchased blue piping
1¼ yards (¾"-wide) white gathered lace edging
1 (11" x 10¼") piece of polyester fleece
1⅛ yards (¼"-wide) white satin picot ribbon
Dressmakers' pen

INSTRUCTIONS

All seam allowances are ¼".

1. With design centered, trim Lugana to 8½" x 7¾". From pindot, cut 1 (11" x 10¼") piece for backing; also cut 2 (8½" x 1¾") strips and 2 (10¼" x 1¾") strips for border. From piping, cut 2 (8½") lengths and 2 (7¾") lengths.

2. To make top of wall hanging: With right sides facing and raw edges aligned, sew 2 (7¾") piping lengths to sides of design piece and then 2 (8½") piping lengths to top and bottom.

Use dressmakers' pen to mark center of 1 long edge of each border strip and center of each edge of design piece. With right sides facing, raw edges aligned, and center marks matching, sew short border strips to top and bottom of design piece and then long border strips to sides, sewing along stitching line of piping.

3. With right sides facing and raw edges aligned, sew straight edge of lace to border, easing in fullness around corners.

4. Stack fleece, top (right side up), and backing (right side down). Stitch, leaving an opening for turning. Clip corners; turn. Slipstitch opening closed.

5. Cut ribbon into 4 equal lengths and tie into 4 bows. Tack 1 bow to each corner of piping.

A friend is worth

a thousand stitches

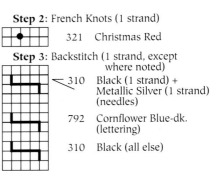

DMC Colors
(used for sample)

Step 1: Cross-stitch (2 strands)

−			White
II		318	Steel Gray-lt.
O		321	Christmas Red
□		437	Tan-lt.
=		502	Blue Green
5		503	Blue Green-med.
^		504	Blue Green-lt.
V		739	Tan-ultra vy. lt.

+		746	Off White
3		754	Peach-lt.
*		762	Pearl Gray-vy. lt.
/		793	Cornflower Blue-med.
•		794	Cornflower Blue-lt.
I		814	Garnet-dk.
X		816	Garnet
//		841	Beige Brown-lt.
Z		842	Beige Brown-vy. lt.
\		948	Peach-vy. lt.
●		3078	Golden Yellow-vy. lt.

Step 2: French Knots (1 strand)

321 Christmas Red

Step 3: Backstitch (1 strand, except where noted)

310 Black (1 strand) + Metallic Silver (1 strand) (needles)

792 Cornflower Blue-dk. (lettering)

310 Black (all else)

45

Country Children

As youngsters, Clay and Seth, my sons, always leapt at the chance to visit our relatives in rural South Carolina, and I well remember how they flourished out in the country.

Away from city distractions, children become so much more inventive. A trunk filled with musty clothes becomes a treasure trove for a little girl and her dress-up dreams. A clutch of chicks becomes a herd of cattle for a little boy and his cowboy fancies. For imaginative children, even a simple walk through the woods yields a thousand such adventures.

Life in the country teaches children to be resourceful and encourages them to dream. Oddly enough, I realized this, not as a country girl myself, but as the proud mother of two city boys with country roots.

Dolly and I

SAMPLE

Sample in photograph was stitched on ash rose 14-count Aida over 2 threads. Design area is 6⅞″ x 9¼″. Fabric was cut 13″ x 16″.

FABRICS	DESIGN AREAS
11-count	4⅜″ x 5⅞″
14-count	3⅜″ x 5¼″
18-count	2⅝″ x 3⅝″
22-count	2⅛″ x 3″

65
↑
→48

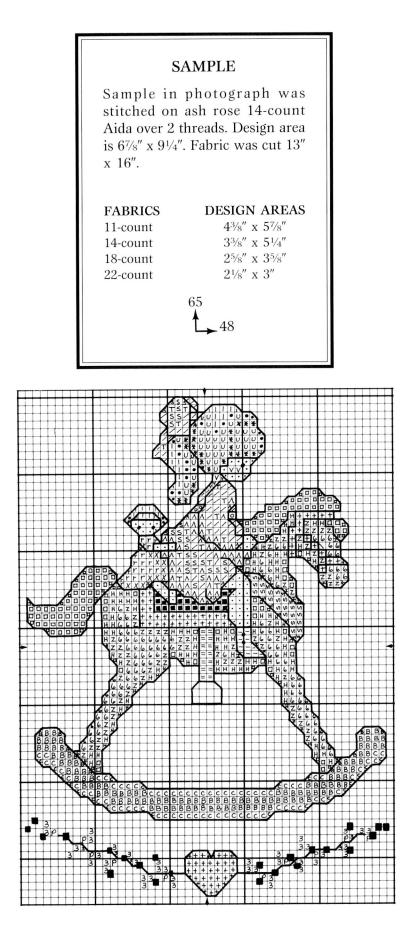

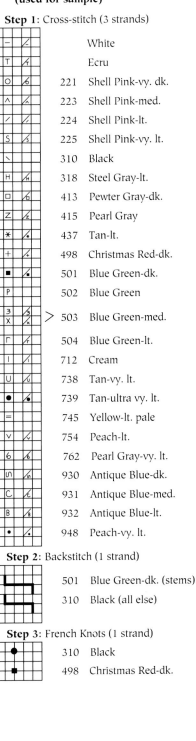

DMC Colors
(used for sample)

Step 1: Cross-stitch (3 strands)

−	╱		White
T	╱		Ecru
O	╱	221	Shell Pink-vy. dk.
^	╱	223	Shell Pink-med.
╱	╱	224	Shell Pink-lt.
S	╱	225	Shell Pink-vy. lt.
\	╱	310	Black
H	╱	318	Steel Gray-lt.
□	╱	413	Pewter Gray-dk.
Z	╱	415	Pearl Gray
*	╱	437	Tan-lt.
+	╱	498	Christmas Red-dk.
■	╱	501	Blue Green-dk.
P	╱	502	Blue Green
3 / X	╱	503	Blue Green-med.
⌐	╱	504	Blue Green-lt.
I	╱	712	Cream
U	╱	738	Tan-vy. lt.
●	╱	739	Tan-ultra vy. lt.
=	╱	745	Yellow-lt. pale
V	╱	754	Peach-lt.
6	╱	762	Pearl Gray-vy. lt.
5	╱	930	Antique Blue-dk.
C	╱	931	Antique Blue-med.
B	╱	932	Antique Blue-lt.
•	╱	948	Peach-vy. lt.

Step 2: Backstitch (1 strand)

	501	Blue Green-dk. (stems)
	310	Black (all else)

Step 3: French Knots (1 strand)

●	310	Black
■	498	Christmas Red-dk.

49

Teddy and Me

SAMPLE

Sample in photograph was stitched on slate 14-count Aida over 2 threads. Design area is 6⅞″ x 9″. Fabric was cut 13″ x 15″.

FABRICS	DESIGN AREAS
11-count	4⅜″ x 5¾″
14-count	3⅜″ x 4½″
18-count	2⅝″ x 3½″
22-count	2⅛″ x 2⅞″

63
↑
→ 48

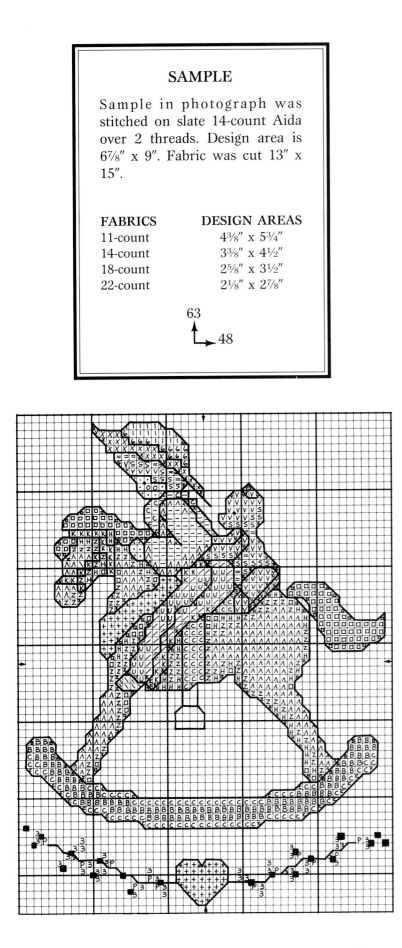

DMC Colors
(used for sample)

Step 1: Cross-stitch (3 strands)

−	∕		White
∖	∕	310	Black
H	∕	318	Steel Gray-lt.
□	∕	413	Pewter Gray-dk.
Z	∕	415	Pearl Gray
=	∕	436	Tan
S	∕	437	Tan-lt.
+	∕	498	Christmas Red-dk.
P		502	Blue Green
3	∕	503	Blue Green-med.
∨	∕	738	Tan-vy. lt.
O	∕	754	Peach-lt.
∧	∕	762	Pearl Gray-vy. lt.
B	∕	814	Garnet-dk.
C	∕	816	Garnet
X	∕	838	Beige Brown-vy. dk.
6	∕	840	Beige Brown-med.
I	∕	841	Beige Brown-lt.
K	∕	930	Antique Blue-dk.
∕	∕	931	Antique Blue-med.
U	∕	932	Antique Blue-lt.
•	∕	948	Peach-vy. lt.

Step 2: Backstitch (1 strand)

	501	Blue Green-dk. (stems)
	310	Black (all else)

Step 3: French Knots (1 strand)

●	310	Black
■	498	Christmas Red-dk.

Hannah and Snowball

SAMPLE

Sample in photograph was stitched on caramel 28-count Annabelle over 2 threads. Design area is 4⅞" x 8". Fabric was cut 11" x 14".

FABRICS	DESIGN AREAS
11-count	6⅛" x 10⅛"
14-count	4⅞" x 8"
18-count	3¾" x 6¼"
22-count	3⅛" x 5⅛"

112
↑
└→ 68

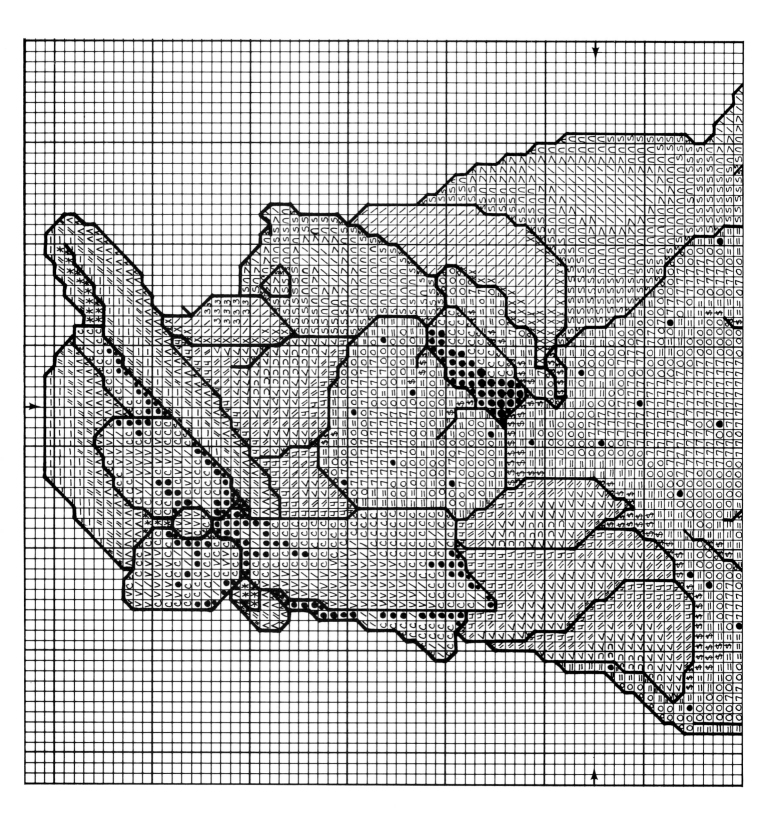

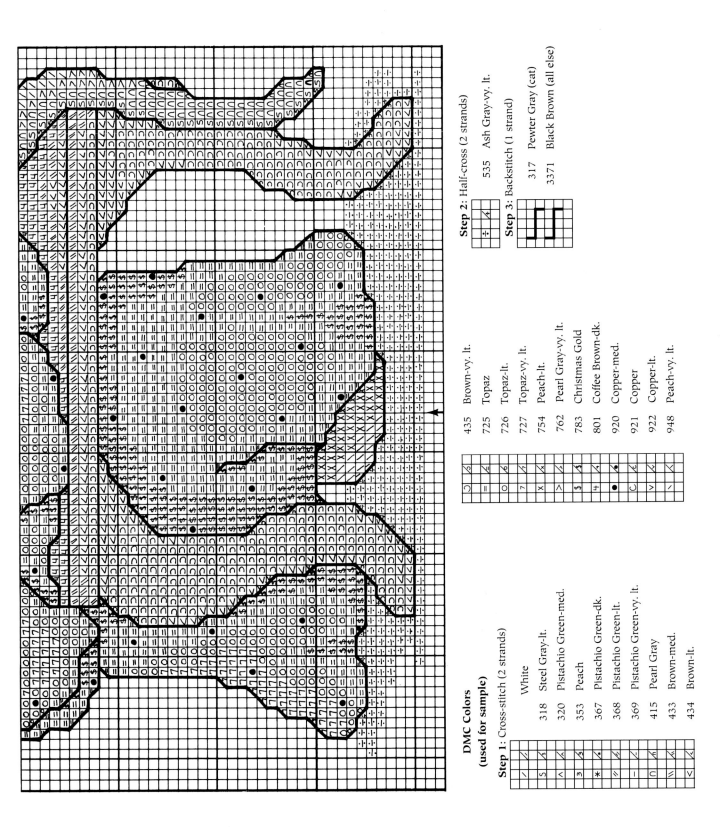

DMC Colors
(used for sample)

Step 1: Cross-stitch (2 strands)

⁄		White
S	↗	318	Steel Gray-lt.
∧	↗	320	Pistachio Green-med.
3	↗	353	Peach
*	↗	367	Pistachio Green-dk.
−		368	Pistachio Green-lt.
∩	↗	369	Pistachio Green-vy. lt.
‖	↗	415	Pearl Gray
∨	↗	433	Brown-med.
	↗	434	Brown-lt.

⊂	↗	435	Brown-vy. lt.
‖	↙	725	Topaz
◯	↗	726	Topaz-lt.
7	↗	727	Topaz-vy. lt.
✕	↙	754	Peach-lt.
>	↗	762	Pearl Gray-vy. lt.
$	↗	783	Christmas Gold
4	↗	801	Coffee Brown-dk.
●		920	Copper-med.
C	↗	921	Copper
∨	↗	922	Copper-lt.
⁄	↗	948	Peach-vy. lt.

Step 2: Half-cross (2 strands)

·		
·	◢	

535 Ash Gray-vy. lt.

Step 3: Backstitch (1 strand)

317 Pewter Gray (cat)
3371 Black Brown (all else)

55

I Love Cross-Stitch

<table>
<tr><td>

SAMPLE

Sample in photograph was stitched on dawn gray 28-count Jubilee over 2 threads. Design area is 7⅜″ x 8⅞″. Fabric was cut 14″ x 15″.

</td><td>

FABRICS
11-count
14-count
18-count
22-count

</td><td>

DESIGN AREAS
9⅜″ x 11⅜″
7⅜″ x 8⅞″
5¾″ x 7″
4⅝″ x 5⅝″

</td><td>

125
103

</td></tr>
</table>

DMC Colors
(used for sample)

Step 1: Cross-stitch (2 strands)

I	⁄		White
Z	⁄	223	Shell Pink-med.
L	⁄	224	Shell Pink-lt.

∩	⁄	225	Shell Pink-vy. lt.
●	⁄	310	Black
⁄		353	Peach
3	⁄	502	Blue Green
5	⁄	519	Sky Blue
P	⁄	646	Beaver Gray-dk.

4	⁄	676	Old Gold-lt.
6	⁄	677	Old Gold-vy. lt.
7	⁄	739	Tan-ultra vy. lt.
e	⁄	747	Sky Blue-vy. lt.
O	⁄	754	Peach-lt.

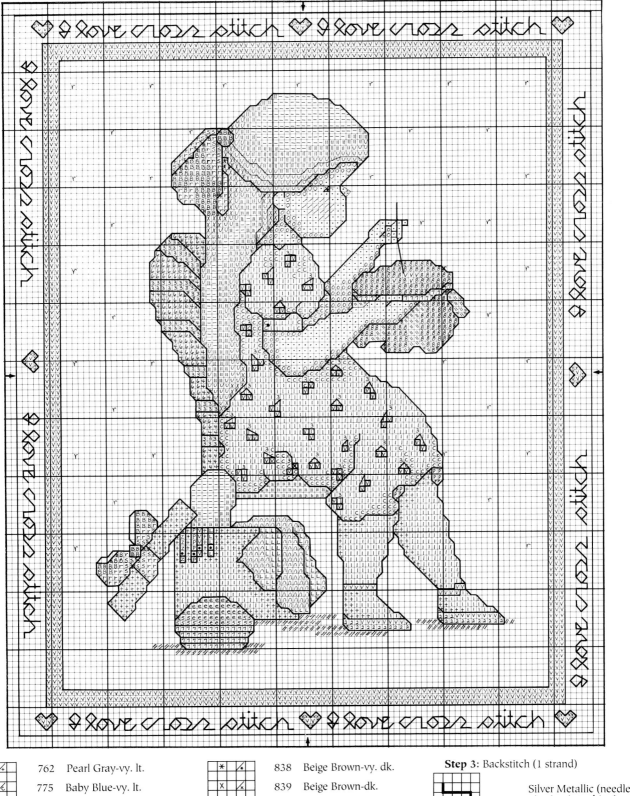

+	⁄	762	Pearl Gray-vy. lt.	
C	⁄	775	Baby Blue-vy. lt.	
S	⁄	792	Cornflower Blue-dk.	
⌐	⁄	793	Cornflower Blue-med.	
B	⁄	794	Cornflower Blue-lt.	
2	⁄	814	Garnet-dk.	
V	⁄	816	Garnet	
\\	⁄	827	Blue-vy. lt.	
8	⁄	828	Blue-ultra vy. lt.	

*	⁄	838	Beige Brown-vy. dk.	
X	⁄	839	Beige Brown-dk.	
U	⁄	840	Beige Brown-med.	
‖	⁄	841	Beige Brown-lt.	
–	⁄	842	Beige Brown-vy. lt.	
•	⁄	948	Peach-vy. lt.	

Step 2: Half-cross (2 strands)

⁄⁄	⁄	646 Beaver Gray-dk.

Step 3: Backstitch (1 strand)

Silver Metallic (needle, pins in pincushion)

816 Garnet (thread in needle)

310 Black (all else)

Step 4: French Knots (1 strand)

● 310 Black

57

Friends Forever

SAMPLE

Sample in photograph was stitched on ivory 14-count Aida over 1 thread. Design area is 4⅛" x 5⅝". Fabric was cut 11" x 12".

FABRICS	DESIGN AREAS
11-count	5⅛" x 7⅛"
18-count	3⅛" x 4⅜"
22-count	2½" x 3½"

79 →
↳ 57

DMC Colors (used for sample)

Step 1: Cross-stitch (2 strands)

		Color
＼ ↗		White
X, * ↗	> 223	Shell Pink-med.
/ ↗	224	Shell Pink-lt.
7, − ↗	> 225	Shell Pink-vy. lt.
S ↗	501	Blue Green-dk.
V ↗	502	Blue Green
• ↗	503	Blue Green-med.
C ↗	754	Peach-lt.
∧ ↗	762	Pearl Gray-vy. lt.
+ ↗	841	Beige Brown-lt.
O ↗	842	Beige Brown-vy. lt.

Step 2: Backstitch (1 strand)

	502	Blue Green (lettering)
	3371	Black Brown (all else)

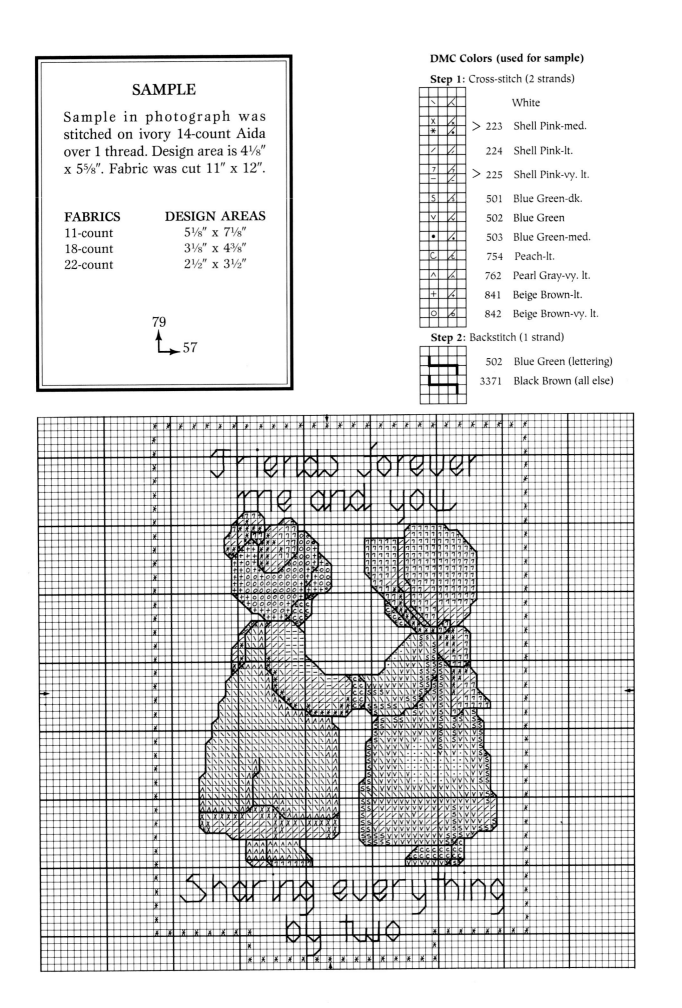

Friends forever
me and you

Sharing everything
by two

Tubby Time

SAMPLES

Samples in photograph were stitched on ivory 14-count Aida over 1 thread. Design areas are 4⅞" x 5¼" for the girl, 5⅜" x 5¾" for the boy. Fabric was cut 12" x 12" for each.

Girl

FABRICS	DESIGN AREAS
11-count	6¼" x 6⅝"
18-count	3⅞" x 4"
22-count	3⅛" x 3⅜"

73
⤷ 69

Boy

FABRICS	DESIGN AREAS
11-count	6⅞" x 7¼"
18-count	4⅛" x 4½"
22-count	3⅜" x 3⅝"

80
⤷ 75

DMC Colors
(used for sample)

Step 1: Cross-stitch (2 strands)

•		∕		White

X					301	Mahogany-med.
÷		4		353	Peach
I				414	Steel Gray-dk.
+				433	Brown-med.
3				612	Drab Brown-med.
C				646	Beaver Gray-dk.
∧				648	Beaver Gray-lt.
∕				743	Yellow-med.
●				745	Yellow-lt. pale
L				754	Peach-lt.
Z				775	Baby Blue-vy. lt.
∇				801	Coffee Brown-dk.
S				911	Emerald Green-med.
O				922	Copper-lt.
\				991	Aquamarine-dk.
□				992	Aquamarine
K				993	Aquamarine-lt.

Step 2: Backstitch (1 strand)

301 Mahogany-med. (hair)

414 Steel Gray-dk. (perfume bottle, nail on wall, bathtub)

422 Hazel Nut Brown-lt. (wall)

433 Brown-med. (shelf, towel rack, baseboards, mouse's hole)

518 Wedgewood-lt. (bubbles, box of soap)

612 Drab Brown-med. (girl's body and face, towel, doll's body and face, rug)

646 Beaver Gray-dk. (mouse)

817 Coral Red-vy. dk. (girl's mouth)

911 Emerald Green-med. (flower stem)

991 Aquamarine-dk. (bandanna, slippers)

Step 3: Long Loose Stitch (1 strand)

414 Steel Gray-dk. (picture wire)

433 Brown-med. (floorboards)

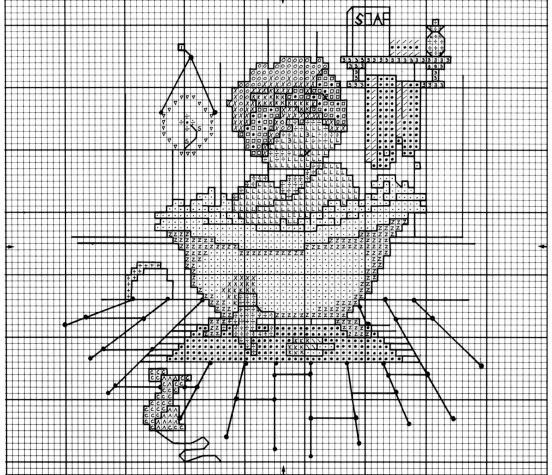

DMC Colors
(used for sample)

Step 1: Cross-stitch (2 strands)

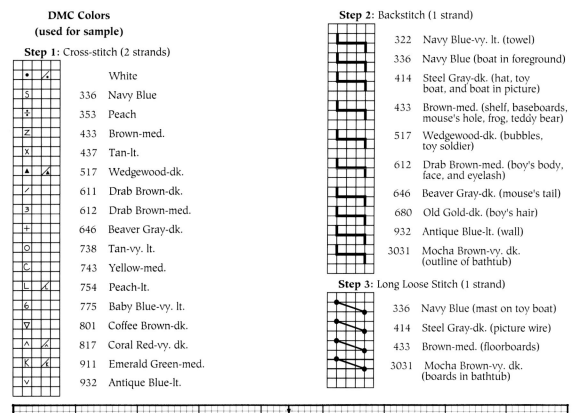

	White
336	Navy Blue
353	Peach
433	Brown-med.
437	Tan-lt.
517	Wedgewood-dk.
611	Drab Brown-dk.
612	Drab Brown-med.
646	Beaver Gray-dk.
738	Tan-vy. lt.
743	Yellow-med.
754	Peach-lt.
775	Baby Blue-vy. lt.
801	Coffee Brown-dk.
817	Coral Red-vy. dk.
911	Emerald Green-med.
932	Antique Blue-lt.

Step 2: Backstitch (1 strand)

322	Navy Blue-vy. lt. (towel)
336	Navy Blue (boat in foreground)
414	Steel Gray-dk. (hat, toy boat, and boat in picture)
433	Brown-med. (shelf, baseboards, mouse's hole, frog, teddy bear)
517	Wedgewood-dk. (bubbles, toy soldier)
612	Drab Brown-med. (boy's body, face, and eyelash)
646	Beaver Gray-dk. (mouse's tail)
680	Old Gold-dk. (boy's hair)
932	Antique Blue-lt. (wall)
3031	Mocha Brown-vy. dk. (outline of bathtub)

Step 3: Long Loose Stitch (1 strand)

336	Navy Blue (mast on toy boat)
414	Steel Gray-dk. (picture wire)
433	Brown-med. (floorboards)
3031	Mocha Brown-vy. dk. (boards in bathtub)

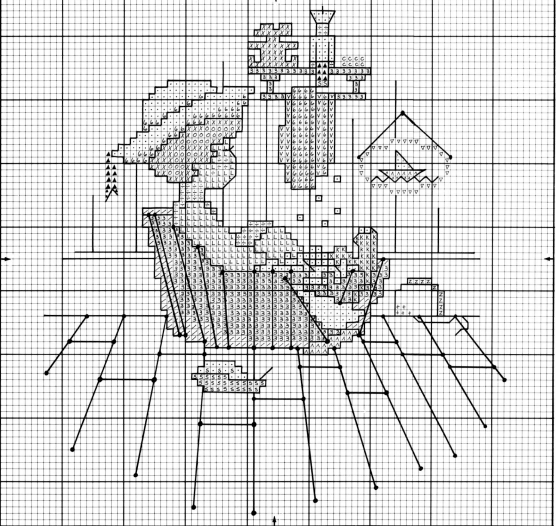

Country Christmas

When I think of Christmas, I think first of Christmases past, when the sights and sounds of that magical day were impressed upon my memory.

Every year, the family gathered at Mom Berta (my grandmother) and Grandpa's small country home in Dillon, South Carolina. Mothers bustled about the kitchen, busy filling the air with laughter and delicious aromas. Fathers gathered around the old wood stove, debating everything from world politics to college football. A tribe of children, from toddlers to teens, dashed to and fro in eager anticipation of Christmas dinner.

Many of my holiday designs were born from these fond reminiscences. Perhaps one of my cross-stitch creations will stir a memory or two for you.

I Believe in
Santa Claus

MATERIALS

Completed cross-stitch on ivory 28-count Jubilee; matching thread
⅝ yard (45″-wide) maroon plaid; matching thread
⅛ yard (45″-wide) forest green fabric; matching thread
1⅜ yards of medium cording
Dressmakers' pen
Stuffing

INSTRUCTIONS

All seam allowances are ¼″.

1. With design centered, trim Jubilee to 10″ x 12½″. From plaid, cut 1 (10″ x 12½″) piece for pillow back and 3 (35″ x 6½″) strips for ruffle. From forest green fabric, cut 1½″-wide bias strips, piecing as needed to equal 47″. With bias strip and cording, make 47″ of corded piping.

2. With right sides facing and raw edges aligned, pin piping around all edges of pillow front. Baste piping in place.

3. To make ruffle: With right sides facing and raw edges aligned, stitch ends of 3 maroon plaid strips together to make 1 (104″ x 6½″) strip. Press seams open. With right sides facing and raw edges aligned, fold strip in half lengthwise to measure 3¼″ wide; stitch ends. Turn and press. Run gathering threads along raw edges through both layers. Mark ruffle at 23″, 52″, and 75″. Beginning at bottom left-hand corner, pin ruffle to right side of pillow front, aligning raw edges and placing marks at corners. Gather ruffle to fit. Stitch along stitching line of piping, through all layers.

4. Place pillow back over front, with right sides facing, raw edges aligned, and piping and ruffle toward center. Stitch, leaving an opening on 1 side. Trim corners and turn. Stuff firmly. Slip-stitch opening closed.

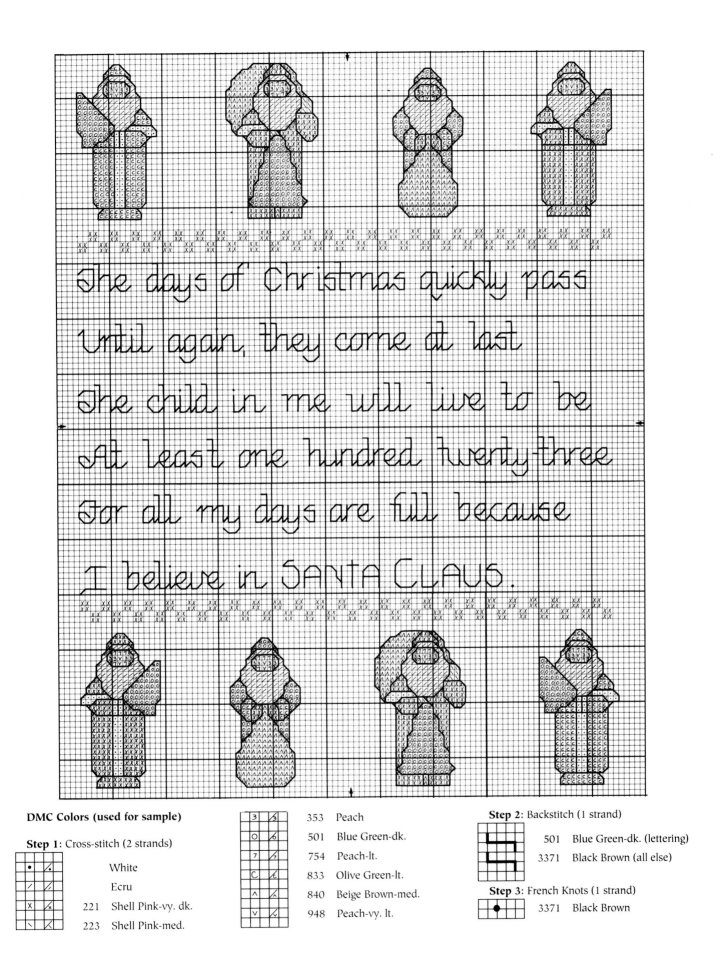

The days of Christmas quickly pass

Until again, they come at last

The child in me will live to be

At least one hundred twenty-three

For all my days are full because

I believe in SANTA CLAUS.

DMC Colors (used for sample)

Step 1: Cross-stitch (2 strands)

•	/		White
/	/		Ecru
X	x	221	Shell Pink-vy. dk.
\	\	223	Shell Pink-med.

3	3	353	Peach
O	6	501	Blue Green-dk.
7	/	754	Peach-lt.
C	c	833	Olive Green-lt.
^	^	840	Beige Brown-med.
V	V	948	Peach-vy. lt.

Step 2: Backstitch (1 strand)

	501	Blue Green-dk. (lettering)
	3371	Black Brown (all else)

Step 3: French Knots (1 strand)

	•	3371	Black Brown

Chimney Socks

SAMPLES

Samples in photograph were stitched on tan 20-count Jobelan over 2 threads. Design area is 7⅝" x 13" for each. Fabric was cut 14" x 19" for each.

FABRICS	DESIGN AREAS
11-count	6⅞" x 11⅞"
14-count	5½" x 9¼"
18-count	4¼" x 7¼"
22-count	3½" x 5⅞"

130
76

MATERIALS (for 1 chimney sock)

Completed cross-stitch on tan 20-count Jobelan; matching thread
½ yard (45"-wide) tan fabric; matching thread
1 (10" x 17") piece of fusible interfacing
1 yard (¼"-wide) purchased metallic gold piping
4½ yards (⅜"-wide) maroon satin ribbon
4½ yards (¼"-wide) dark green satin ribbon
Tracing paper for pattern
Dressmakers' pen

INSTRUCTIONS

All seam allowances are ¼".

1. Enlarge chimney sock on grid to make a full-size pattern; cut out. Place pattern over stitched design, with design centered vertically and horizontally; cut out sock front. From tan fabric, cut 3 sock pieces (1 for back and 2 for lining).

2. Iron interfacing to wrong side of front. Trim excess interfacing.

3. With right sides facing and raw edges aligned, stitch piping along side and bottom edges of front. With right sides facing and raw edges aligned, stitch front to back, sewing along stitching line of piping and leaving top edge open. Clip curves and turn.

4. To make lining: With right sides facing and raw edges aligned, stitch together 2 lining pieces, leaving top edge open and a large opening in side seam above bottom edge. Clip curves. Do not turn. With right sides facing, slide lining over sock, matching side seams. Stitch around top edge of sock. Turn through opening in lining. Slip-stitch opening closed. Tuck lining inside sock.

5. For hanger, cut 1 (18″) length each from maroon and dark green ribbons; tack ends of ribbons to either side of sock back, just behind piping and about ½″ below top edge. For bows, cut remaining ribbon into 36″ lengths. Handling 2 lengths of each color as a single unit, tie 1 (4″) bow. Repeat. Tack bows over ends of hanger.

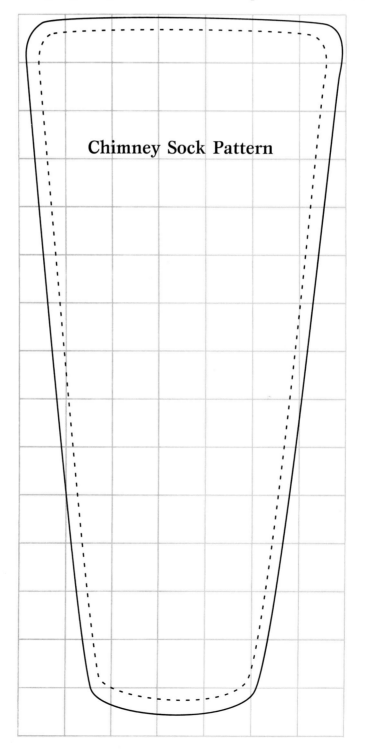

Chimney Sock Pattern

Each square equals 1″.

DMC Colors
(used for sample)

Step 1: Cross-stitch (2 strands)

•	⁄		White
∧	⁄	317	Pewter Gray
⊃	⁄	318	Steel Gray-lt.
＼	⁄	321	Christmas Red
З	⁄	353	Peach
Ɛ	⁄	413	Pewter Gray-dk.
4	⁄	414	Steel Gray-dk.
O	⁄	498	Christmas Red-dk.
⁄	⁄	500	Blue Green-vy. dk.
‖	⁄	501	Blue Green-dk.
>	⁄	502	Blue Green
*	⁄	738	Tan-vy. lt.
U	⁄	739	Tan-ultra vy. lt.
7	⁄	754	Peach-lt.
C	⁄	762	Pearl Gray-vy. lt.
◤		798	Delft-dk.
X	⁄	815	Garnet-med.
8	⁄	838	Beige Brown-vy. dk.
9	⁄	839	Beige Brown-dk.
‖	⁄	840	Beige Brown-med.
<	⁄	842	Beige Brown-vy. lt.
⁄	⁄	902	Garnet-vy. dk.
–	⁄	948	Peach-vy. lt.
Z	⁄	002HL	Gold Balger blending filament

Step 2: Backstitch (1 strand)

	798	Delft-dk. (eye)
	002HL	Gold Balger blending filament (epaulet, fringe)
	3371	Black Brown (all else)

Step 3: French Knots (1 strand)

●	002HL	Gold Balger blending filament

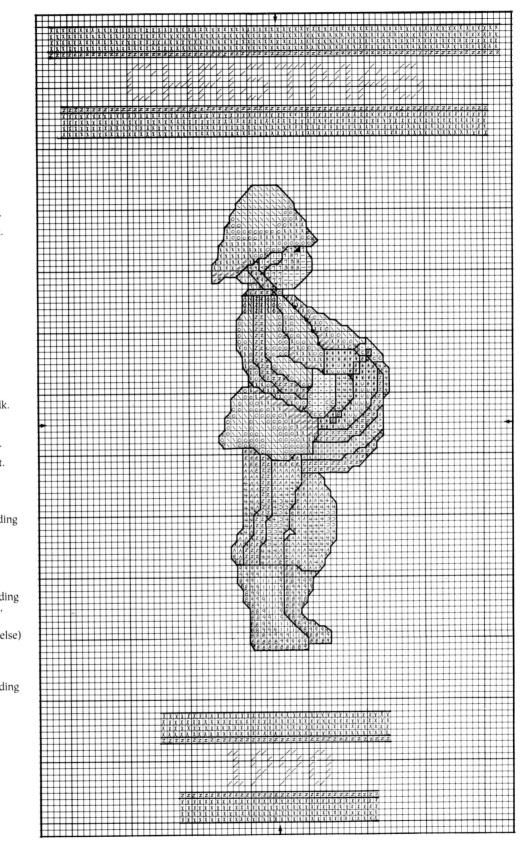

71

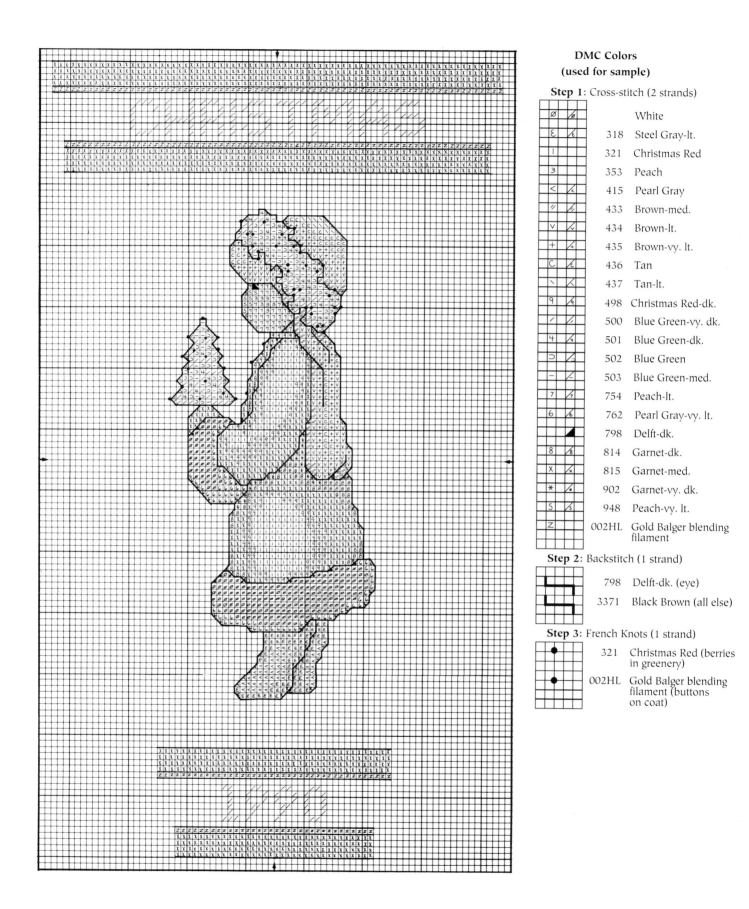

DMC Colors
(used for sample)

Step 1: Cross-stitch (2 strands)

Ø	Ø		White
ε	ε	318	Steel Gray-lt.
I	I	321	Christmas Red
3		353	Peach
<	<	415	Pearl Gray
//	//	433	Brown-med.
V	V	434	Brown-lt.
+	+	435	Brown-vy. lt.
C	C	436	Tan
\	\	437	Tan-lt.
9	9	498	Christmas Red-dk.
/	/	500	Blue Green-vy. dk.
4	4	501	Blue Green-dk.
Ɔ	Ɔ	502	Blue Green
–	–	503	Blue Green-med.
7	7	754	Peach-lt.
6	6	762	Pearl Gray-vy. lt.
	◤	798	Delft-dk.
8	8	814	Garnet-dk.
X	X	815	Garnet-med.
*	*	902	Garnet-vy. dk.
S	S	948	Peach-vy. lt.
Z		002HL	Gold Balger blending filament

Step 2: Backstitch (1 strand)

	798	Delft-dk. (eye)
	3371	Black Brown (all else)

Step 3: French Knots (1 strand)

●	321	Christmas Red (berries in greenery)
●	002HL	Gold Balger blending filament (buttons on coat)

Whirligig Santa

SAMPLE

Sample in photograph was stitched on khaki 18-count Aida over 2 threads. Design area is 6⅝" x 14⅞". Fabric was cut 13" x 21".

FABRICS	DESIGN AREAS
11-count	5½" x 12⅛"
14-count	4¼" x 9⅝"
18-count	3⅜" x 7½"
22-count	2¾" x 6⅛"

134 ↑
→ 60

INSTRUCTIONS

All seam allowances are ¼".

1. With design centered, trim Aida to 8" x 16". From green-and-maroon print, cut 1 (8" x 16") piece for backing. From maroon fabric, cut 1½"-wide bias strips, piecing as needed to equal 69". From this bias strip, cut 1 (19") length for hanging strip. With remaining length of bias strip and medium cording, make 50" of corded piping.

2. With right sides facing and raw edges aligned, stitch piping around all edges of design piece.

3. To make hanging strip: With right sides facing and raw edges aligned, fold 19" bias strip in half lengthwise to measure ¾" wide; stitch along raw edges of long side only. Turn and press. With raw ends of strip aligned with raw edges of piping and strip toward center, pin each end of hanger 1" inside each corner at top of design piece.

4. With right sides facing and raw edges aligned, stitch backing to design piece, sewing along stitching line of piping, catching hanger in seam, and leaving an opening along bottom edge for turning. Trim corners and turn. Slipstitch opening closed.

MATERIALS

Completed cross-stitch on khaki 18-count Aida; matching thread
¼ yard (45"-wide) green-and-maroon print; matching thread
¼ yard (45"-wide) maroon fabric; matching thread
1½ yards of medium cording

73

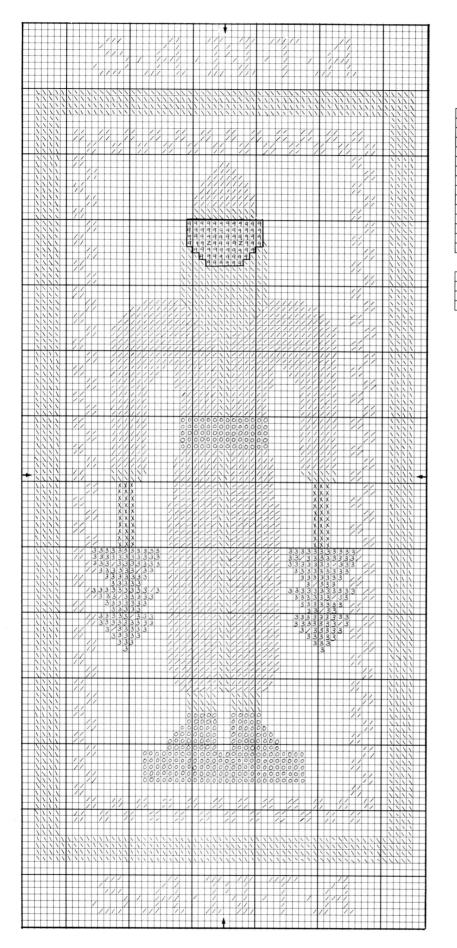

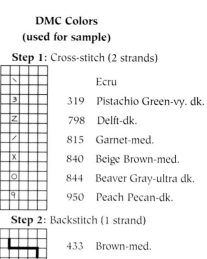

DMC Colors
(used for sample)

Step 1: Cross-stitch (2 strands)

＼		Ecru
3	319	Pistachio Green-vy. dk.
Z	798	Delft-dk.
／	815	Garnet-med.
X	840	Beige Brown-med.
O	844	Beaver Gray-ultra dk.
9	950	Peach Pecan-dk.

Step 2: Backstitch (1 strand)

	433	Brown-med.

Santa and His Little Helper

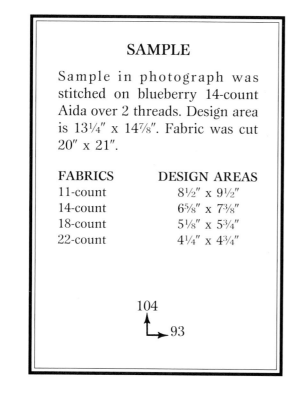

SAMPLE

Sample in photograph was stitched on blueberry 14-count Aida over 2 threads. Design area is 13¼" x 14⅞". Fabric was cut 20" x 21".

FABRICS	DESIGN AREAS
11-count	8½" x 9½"
14-count	6⅝" x 7⅜"
18-count	5⅛" x 5¾"
22-count	4¼" x 4¾"

104
93

MATERIALS

Completed cross-stitch on blueberry 14-count Aida; matching thread

1⅜ yards (45"-wide) maroon miniprint; matching thread

¼ yard (45"-wide) green gingham

¼ yard (45"-wide) green fabric; matching thread

1 (28" x 30½") piece of polyester fleece

Dressmakers' pen

INSTRUCTIONS

All seam allowances are ¼".

1. With design centered, trim Aida to 15" x 17½". From miniprint, cut 1 (28" x 30½") piece for backing; also cut 2 (21" x 4") strips and 2 (30½" x 4") strips for border. From gingham, cut 2 (19" x 1½") strips and 2 (23½" x 1½") strips for border. From green fabric, cut 2 (17½" x 2½") strips and 2 (19" x 2½") strips for border.

2. To make top of wall hanging: Use dressmakers' pen to mark center of 1 long edge of each green border strip and center of each edge of design piece. With right sides facing, raw edges aligned, and center marks matching, sew short green strips to sides of design piece and then long green strips to top and bottom. Mark and sew gingham border strips to green border strips in same manner, except first sew short strips to top and bottom and then long strips to sides. Mark and sew miniprint border strips to gingham border strips in same manner as gingham strips.

3. Stack fleece, top (right side up), and backing (right side down). Stitch, leaving an opening for turning. Trim corners and turn. Slipstitch opening closed.

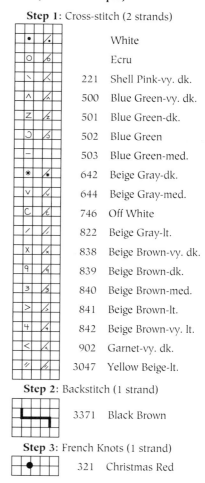

DMC Colors
(used for sample)

Step 1: Cross-stitch (2 strands)

•	∕		White
○	◐		Ecru
\	∠	221	Shell Pink-vy. dk.
^	∠	500	Blue Green-vy. dk.
Z	∠	501	Blue Green-dk.
⊃	◢	502	Blue Green
–	∕	503	Blue Green-med.
*	◢	642	Beige Gray-dk.
v	∠	644	Beige Gray-med.
C	∠	746	Off White
/	∕	822	Beige Gray-lt.
X	∠	838	Beige Brown-vy. dk.
9	◢	839	Beige Brown-dk.
3	∕	840	Beige Brown-med.
>	∠	841	Beige Brown-lt.
4	∕	842	Beige Brown-vy. lt.
<	∠	902	Garnet-vy. dk.
∕∕	∕	3047	Yellow Beige-lt.

Step 2: Backstitch (1 strand)

L	3371	Black Brown

Step 3: French Knots (1 strand)

●	321	Christmas Red

76

I Will Honor Christmas

SAMPLE

Sample in photograph was stitched on oatmeal 18-count Rustico Aida over 2 threads. Design area is 14⅜" x 7⅜". Fabric was cut 21" x 14".

FABRICS	DESIGN AREAS
11-count	11⅞" x 6"
14-count	9¼" x 4¾"
18-count	7¼" x 3⅝"
22-count	5⅞" x 3"

66
↑
└→130

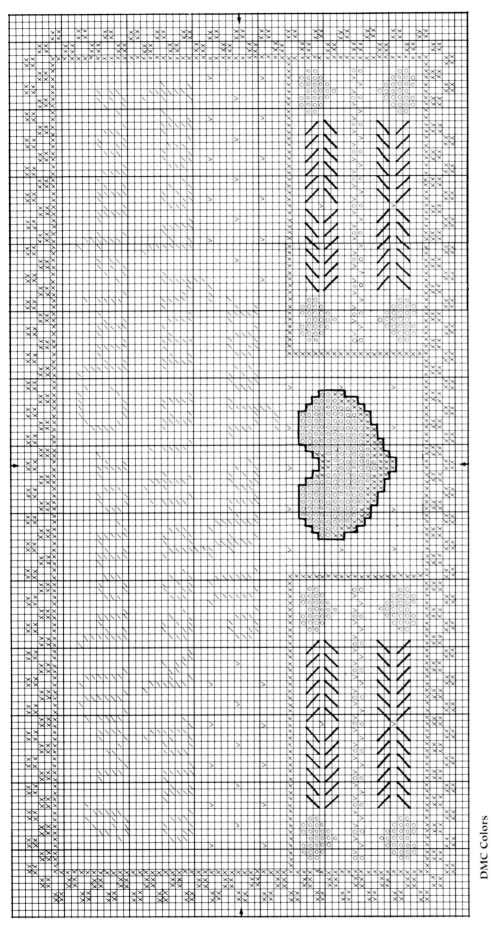

DMC Colors
(used for sample)

Step 1: Cross-stitch (2 strands)

>	Ecru
816	Garnet
902	Garnet-vy. dk.
924	Slate Green-vy. dk.

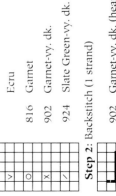

Step 2: Backstitch (1 strand)

902	Garnet-vy. dk. (heart)
	Ecru (all else)

Christmas Stockings

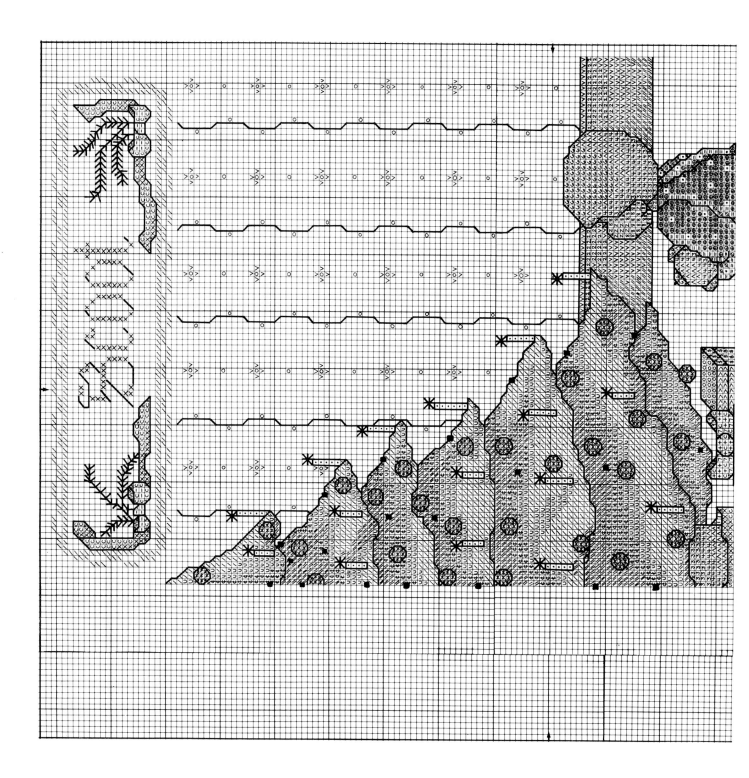

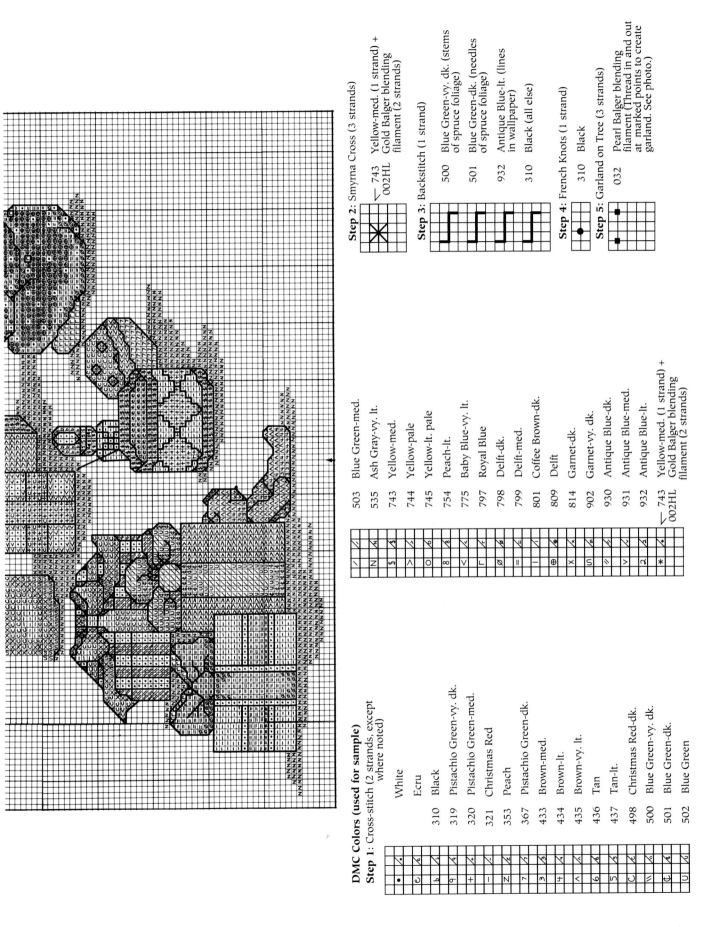

DMC Colors (used for sample)

Step 1: Cross-stitch (2 strands, except where noted)

Symbol	No.	Color
•		White
e		Ecru
b	310	Black
9	319	Pistachio Green-vy. dk.
+	320	Pistachio Green-med.
–	321	Christmas Red
N	353	Peach
7	367	Pistachio Green-dk.
3	433	Brown-med.
+	434	Brown-lt.
<	435	Brown-vy. lt.
6	436	Tan
5	437	Tan-lt.
C	498	Christmas Red-dk.
\	500	Blue Green-vy. dk.
C	501	Blue Green-dk.
U	502	Blue Green

Symbol	No.	Color
/	503	Blue Green-med.
N	535	Ash Gray-vy. lt.
$	743	Yellow-med.
>	744	Yellow-pale
O	745	Yellow-lt. pale
8	754	Peach-lt.
V	775	Baby Blue-vy. lt.
r	797	Royal Blue
Ø	798	Delft-dk.
=	799	Delft-med.
I	801	Coffee Brown-dk.
⊕	809	Delft
X	814	Garnet-dk.
S	902	Garnet-vy. dk.
⫽	930	Antique Blue-dk.
V	931	Antique Blue-med.
2	932	Antique Blue-lt.
*	743 / 002HL	Yellow-med. (1 strand) + Gold Balger blending filament (2 strands)

Step 2: Smyrna Cross (3 strands)

Symbol	No.	Color
✳	743 / 002HL	Yellow-med. (1 strand) + Gold Balger blending filament (2 strands)

Step 3: Backstitch (1 strand)

500	Blue Green-vy. dk. (stems of spruce foliage)
501	Blue Green-dk. (needles of spruce foliage)
932	Antique Blue-lt. (lines in wallpaper)
310	Black (all else)

Step 4: French Knots (1 strand)

Symbol	No.	Color
●	310	Black

Step 5: Garland on Tree (3 strands)

032	Pearl Balger blending filament (Thread in and out at marked points to create garland. See photo.)

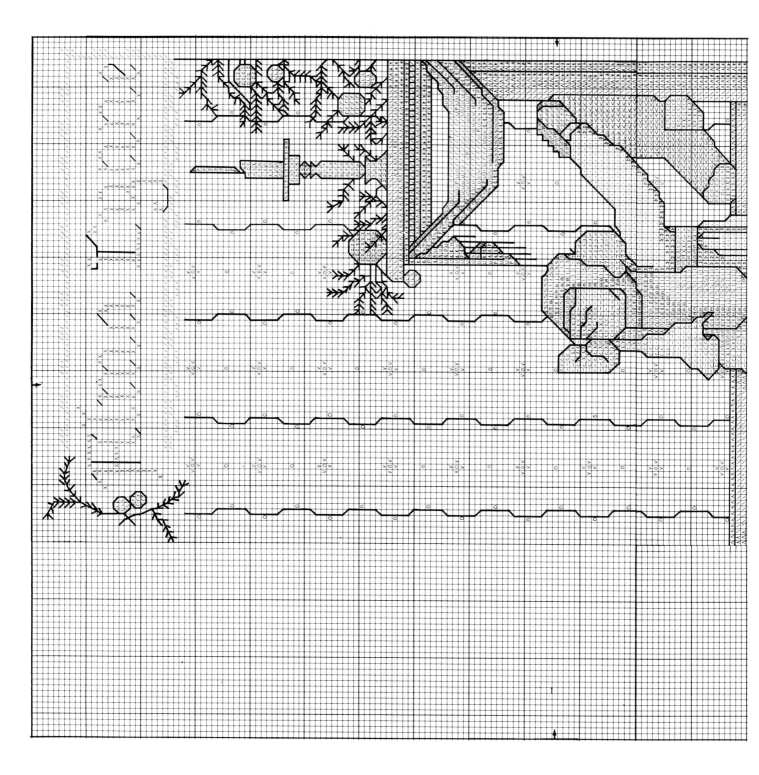

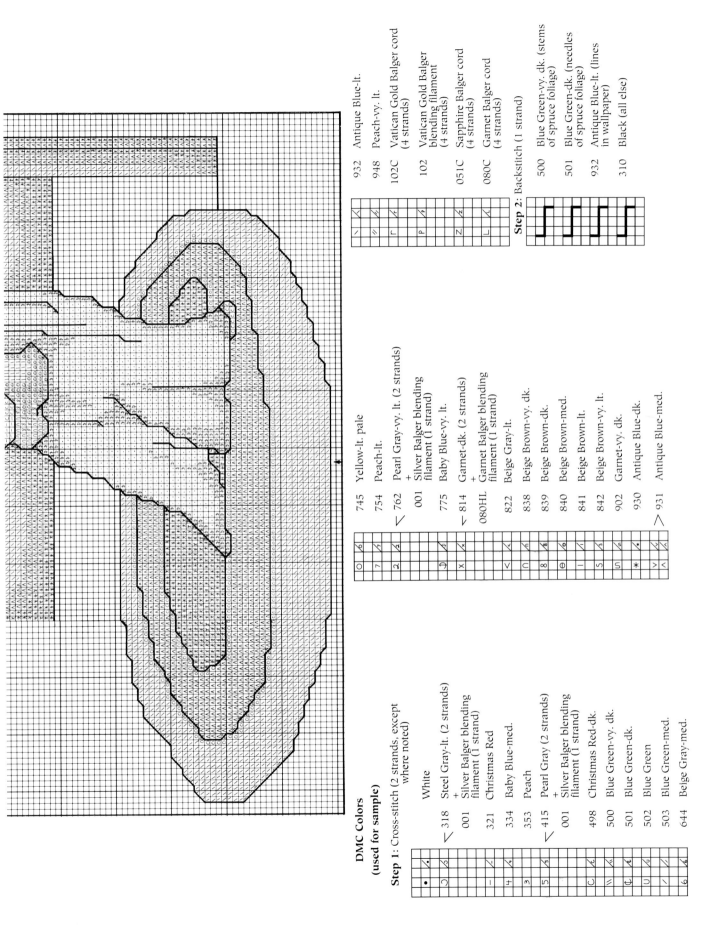

DMC Colors
(used for sample)

Step 1: Cross-stitch (2 strands, except where noted)

•	White
∨ 318	Steel Gray-lt. (2 strands) +
001	Silver Balger blending filament (1 strand)
321	Christmas Red
334	Baby Blue-med.
353	Peach
∨ 415	Pearl Gray (2 strands) +
001	Silver Balger blending filament (1 strand)
498	Christmas Red-dk.
500	Blue Green-vy. dk.
501	Blue Green-dk.
502	Blue Green
503	Blue Green-med.
644	Beige Gray-med.

745	Yellow-lt. pale
754	Peach-lt.
∨ 762	Pearl Gray-vy. lt. (2 strands) +
001	Silver Balger blending filament (1 strand)
775	Baby Blue-vy. lt.
∨ 814	Garnet-dk. (2 strands) +
080HL	Garnet Balger blending filament (1 strand)
822	Beige Gray-lt.
838	Beige Brown-vy. dk.
839	Beige Brown-dk.
840	Beige Brown-med.
841	Beige Brown-lt.
842	Beige Brown-vy. lt.
902	Garnet-vy. dk.
930	Antique Blue-dk.
> 931	Antique Blue-med.

932	Antique Blue-lt.
948	Peach-vy. lt.
102C	Vatican Gold Balger cord (4 strands)
102	Vatican Gold Balger blending filament (4 strands)
051C	Sapphire Balger cord (4 strands)
080C	Garnet Balger cord (4 strands)

Step 2: Backstitch (1 strand)

500	Blue Green-vy. dk. (stems of spruce foliage)
501	Blue Green-dk. (needles of spruce foliage)
932	Antique Blue-lt. (lines in wallpaper)
310	Black (all else)

85

MATERIALS (for 1 stocking)

Completed cross-stitch on ivory 21-count
  Glenshee Linen; matching thread
¾ yard of red moiré taffeta
½ yard (45″-wide) red fabric for lining
2 yards of small cording
1 (17″ x 25″) piece of fusible interfacing
1 5″ piece (⅜″-wide) white satin picot ribbon
Tracing paper for pattern
Dressmakers' pen

INSTRUCTIONS

All seam allowances are ¼″.

1. Enlarge stocking on grid to make a full-size
pattern; cut out. Place pattern over stitched design, with top edge of pattern 1¼″ above top row
of border design and with design centered horizontally; cut out stocking front. From red moiré
taffeta, cut out stocking back; also cut 1¼″-wide
bias strips, piecing as needed to equal 65″. From
red lining fabric, cut 2 stocking pieces. With bias
strip and cording, make 65″ of corded piping.

2. Iron interfacing to wrong side of stocking
front. Trim excess interfacing.

3. With right sides facing and raw edges aligned,
stitch piping around all edges of stocking front.
With right sides facing and raw edges aligned,
stitch back to front, sewing along stitching line of
piping and leaving top edge open. Clip curves
and turn.

4. Fold ribbon in half to make a 2½″ hanger
loop. With raw edges aligned and loop down, pin
loop to right side of stocking back near right
seam.

5. To make lining: With right sides facing and
raw edges aligned, stitch lining pieces together,
leaving top edge open and a large opening in side
seam above heel. Clip curves. Do not turn. With
right sides facing, slide lining over stocking,
matching side seams. Stitch around top edge of
stocking, sewing along stitching line of piping
and catching ends of hanger loop in seam. Turn
stocking through opening in lining. Slipstitch
opening closed. Tuck lining inside stocking.

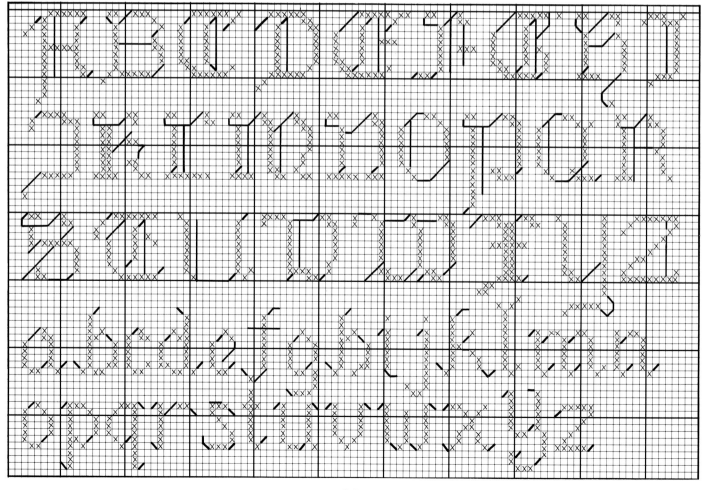

Each square equals 1″.

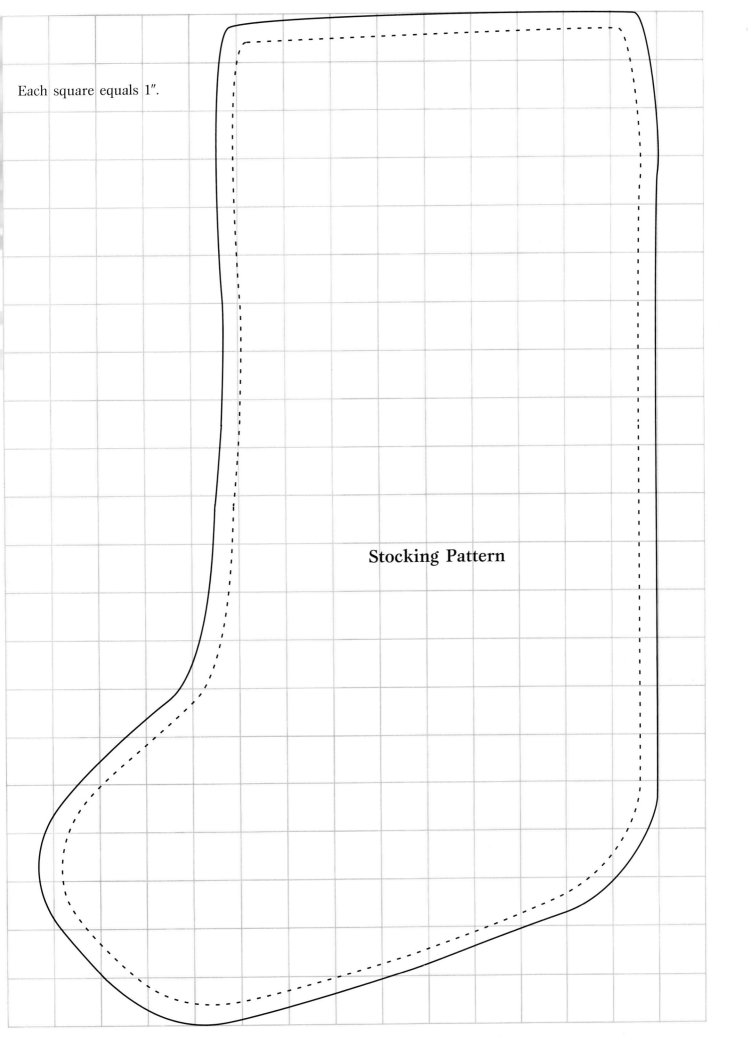

Stocking Pattern

Santa's Here!

DMC Colors
(used for sample)

Step 1: Cross-stitch (2 strands)

/	/		White
H	н		Ecru
b	b	311	Navy Blue-med.
Θ	6	312	Navy Blue-lt.
II	ıı	318	Steel Gray-lt.
∩	n	322	Navy Blue-vy. lt.
L	∠	336	Navy Blue
3	3	353	Peach
W	w	414	Steel Gray-dk.
4	4	415	Pearl Gray
>	>	433	Brown-med.
<	<	434	Brown-lt.
Ø	Ø	435	Brown-vy. lt.
6	6	436	Tan
y	y	437	Tan-lt.
C	C	498	Christmas Red-dk.
\\	\\		
*	*	500	Blue Green-vy. dk.

^	^		
=	=	501	Blue Green-dk.
Z	z		
U	U	502	Blue Green
Ɔ	Ɔ	503	Blue Green-med.
:	:	676	Old Gold-lt.
e	e	680	Old Gold-dk.
f	f	729	Old Gold-med.
$	$	746	Off White
7	7	754	Peach-lt.
S	S	762	Pearl Gray-vy. lt.
Γ	Γ	801	Coffee Brown-dk.
//	//	814	Garnet-dk.
V	V	816	Garnet

B	B	838	Beige Brown-vy. dk.
9	9	839	Beige Brown-dk.
N	N	840	Beige Brown-med.
–	–	841	Beige Brown-lt.
X	X	902	Garnet-vy. dk.
Ɛ	Ɛ	928	Slate Green-lt.
3	3	939	Navy Blue-vy. dk.
\	\	948	Peach-vy. lt.
5	5	3046	Yellow Beige-med.
x	x	3047	Yellow Beige-lt.
8	8	3328	Salmon-dk.
●	●	3371	Black Brown

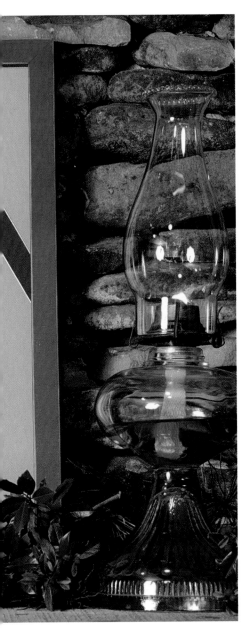

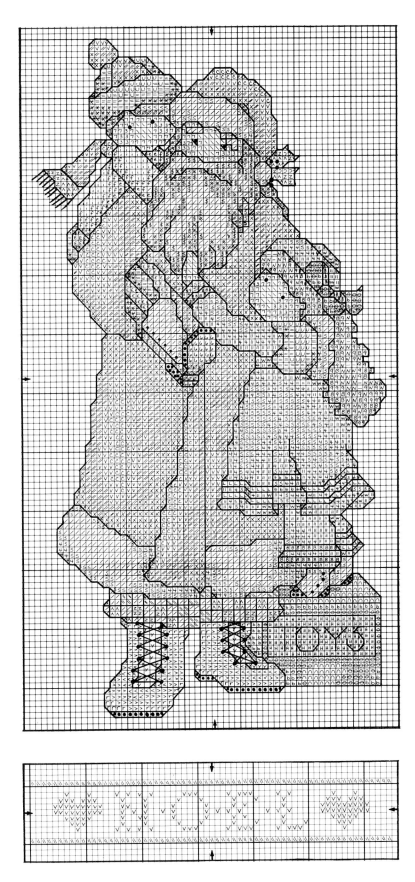

Step 2: Backstitch (1 strand)

434	Brown-lt. (Santa's hair, beard)
902	Garnet-vy. dk. ("Toys")
3371	Black Brown (fringe on scarf)
310	Black (all else)

Step 3: French Knots (1 strand)

498	Christmas Red-dk. (holly)
3371	Black Brown (eyes, girl's boots)

Step 4: Long Loose Stitch (1 strand)

310	Black (Santa's shoelaces)

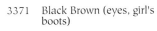

Holiday Goose

SAMPLE	FABRICS	DESIGN AREAS	
Sample in photograph was stitched on ivory 28-count Jubilee over 2 threads. Design area is 9⅛" x 5¼". Fabric was cut 16" x 12".	11-count	11½" x 6¾"	
	14-count	9⅛" x 5¼"	74
	18-count	7" x 4⅛"	↑
	22-count	5¾" x 3⅜"	└→ 127

MATERIALS

Completed cross-stitch on ivory 28-count Jubilee; matching thread
1¼ yards (45"-wide) red pindot; matching thread
¼ yard (45"-wide) yellow fabric; matching thread
1⅞ yards of medium cording
Dressmakers' pen
Stuffing

INSTRUCTIONS

All seam allowances are ¼".

1. With design centered, trim Jubilee to 14" x 10¼". From pindot, cut 1 (17½" x 13¾") piece for pillow back; also cut 2 (13¾" x 2¼") strips and 2 (14" x 2¼") strips for border and 4 (39" x 6½") strips for ruffle. From yellow fabric, cut

1½″-wide bias strips, piecing as needed to equal 67″. With bias strip and cording, make 67″ of corded piping.

2. To make pillow front: Use dressmakers' pen to mark center of 1 long edge of each pindot border strip and center of each edge of design piece. With right sides facing, raw edges aligned, and center marks matching, sew 14″ border strips to top and bottom of design piece and then 13¾″ border strips to sides.

3. With right sides facing and raw edges aligned, pin piping around all edges of pillow front. Baste piping in place.

4. To make ruffle: With right sides facing and raw edges aligned, stitch ends of 4 (39″ x 6½″)

pindot strips together to make 1 (154½″ x 6½″) strip. Press seams open. With right sides facing and raw edges aligned, fold strip in half lengthwise to measure 3¼″ wide; stitch ends. Turn and press. Run gathering threads along long raw edges through both layers. Mark ruffle at 43″, 77″, and 120″. Beginning at bottom left-hand corner, pin ruffle to right side of pillow front, aligning raw edges and placing marks at corners. Gather ruffle to fit. Stitch along stitching line of piping, through all layers.

5. Place pillow back over front, with right sides facing, raw edges aligned, and piping and ruffle toward center. Stitch, leaving an opening on 1 side. Trim corners and turn. Stuff firmly. Slip-stitch opening closed.

DMC Colors (used for sample)

Step 1: Cross-stitch (2 strands)

		White
■		310 Black
-		321 Christmas Red
b		367 Pistachio Green-dk.
v		415 Pearl Gray
6		436 Tan
7		437 Tan-lt.
/		498 Christmas Red-dk.
Z		680 Old Gold-dk.
\		729 Old Gold-med.
8		738 Tan-vy. lt.
O		762 Pearl Gray-vy. lt.
a		814 Garnet-dk.
C		815 Garnet-med.
K		816 Garnet
U		890 Pistachio Green-ultra dk.
+		902 Garnet-vy. dk.
X		921 Copper
^		922 Copper-lt.
e		930 Antique Blue-dk.
<		931 Antique Blue-med.
•		932 Antique Blue-lt.

Step 2: Backstitch (1 strand)

	310 Black

Step 3: French Knots (1 strand)

●	310 Black

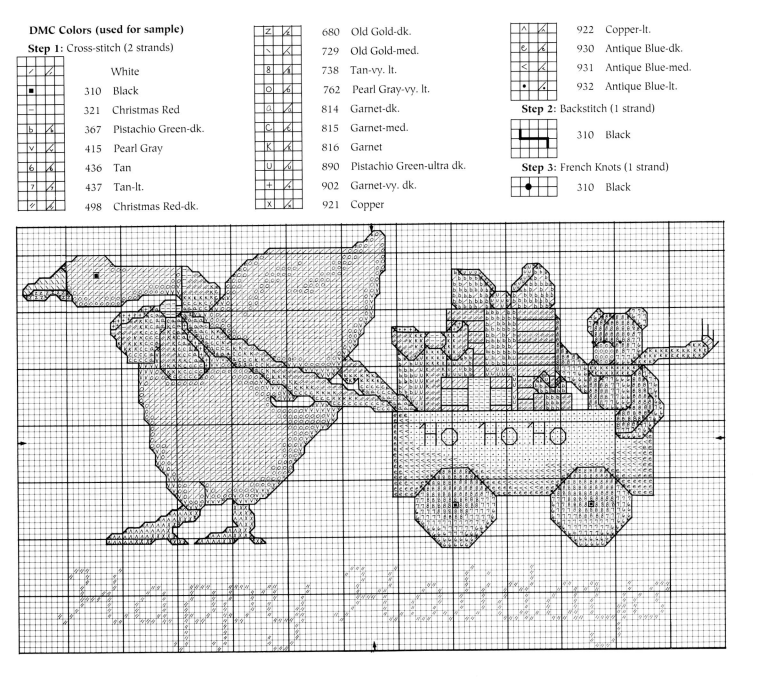

Winter Angel

MATERIALS

Completed cross-stitch on ivory 14-count Soft
  Touch; matching thread
1⅜ yards (45"-wide) maroon fabric; matching
  thread
⅛ yard (45"-wide) dark green fabric
1 (25½" x 32½") piece of polyester fleece
2 yards (1"-wide) ivory satin ribbon; matching
  thread
3 yards (⅜"-wide) maroon grosgrain ribbon
3 yards (⅝"-wide) dark green grosgrain ribbon
Dressmakers' pen

INSTRUCTIONS

All seam allowances are ¼", except where noted.

1. With design centered, trim Soft Touch to
14½" x 21½". From maroon fabric, cut 1 (25½" x
32½") piece for backing; also cut 2 (18½" x 2½")

strips, 2 (21½″ x 2½″) strips, 2 (20″ x 3¼″) strips, and 2 (32½″ x 3¼″) strips for border. From dark green fabric, cut 2 (20″ x 1¼″) strips and 2 (25½″ x 1¼″) for border.

2. To make top of wall hanging: Use dressmakers' pen to mark center of 1 long edge of 2½″-wide maroon border strips and center of each edge of design piece. With right sides facing, raw edges aligned, and center marks matching, first sew long maroon border strips to sides of design piece and then short maroon border strips to top and bottom. Mark and sew green border strips to 2½″-wide maroon border strips in same manner. In same manner, mark and sew 3¼″-wide maroon border strips to green border strips, except first sew short strips to top and bottom and then long strips to sides.

3. Stack top (right side up) on fleece and baste together. Using maroon thread, machine-quilt ¹⁄₁₆″ around outside edge of design piece and on both sides of green border.

4. With right sides facing, stack fleece/top and backing. Stitch, leaving an opening for turning. Clip corners and turn. Slipstitch opening closed.

5. Cut ivory ribbon into 4 equal lengths. Tie each length into a bow. Tack 1 bow to each corner of design piece.

6. Cut each length of grosgrain ribbon in half. Handling 1 maroon and 1 green length of ribbon as 1 unit, tie an 8-looped bow (4 loops on each side of knot). Repeat with 2 remaining lengths of ribbon. Tack 1 bow to each upper corner of green border.

DMC Colors
(used for sample)

Step 1: Cross-stitch (2 strands)

•			White
V		319	Pistachio Green-vy. dk.
/		320	Pistachio Green-med.
3		353	Peach
C		367	Pistachio Green-dk.
^		368	Pistachio Green-lt.
"		433	Brown-med.
4		434	Brown-lt.
<		435	Brown-vy. lt.
⊃		436	Tan
7		437	Tan-lt.
\		498	Christmas Red-dk.
ε		535	Ash Gray-vy. lt.
=		640	Beige Gray-vy. dk.
$		642	Beige Gray-dk.
6		644	Beige Gray-med.
5		754	Peach-lt.
●		792	Cornflower Blue-dk.
>		814	Garnet-dk.
II		815	Garnet-med.
O		816	Garnet
ø			
–		822	Beige Gray-lt.
8		838	Beige Brown-vy. dk.
9		839	Beige Brown-dk.
⊠		840	Beige Brown-med.
L		841	Beige Brown-lt.
⁒		842	Beige Brown-vy. lt.
\\		890	Pistachio Green-ultra dk.
*		902	Garnet-vy. dk.
I		948	Peach-vy. lt.

Step 2: Backstitch (1 strand)

	433	Brown-med. (hair, wings)
	434	Brown-lt. (eyes, face, hands, feet)
	890	Pistachio Green-ultra dk. (holly)
	3371	Black Brown (dress, basket, bow, shoes)

Step 3: French Knots (1 strand)

●	498	Christmas Red-dk.*
●	815	Garnet-med.*
●	816	Garnet*

* Alternate colors as desired.

Kris Kringle

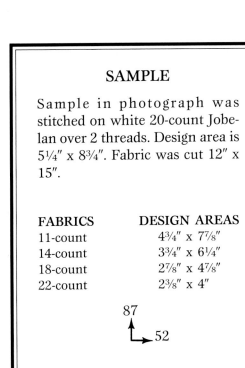

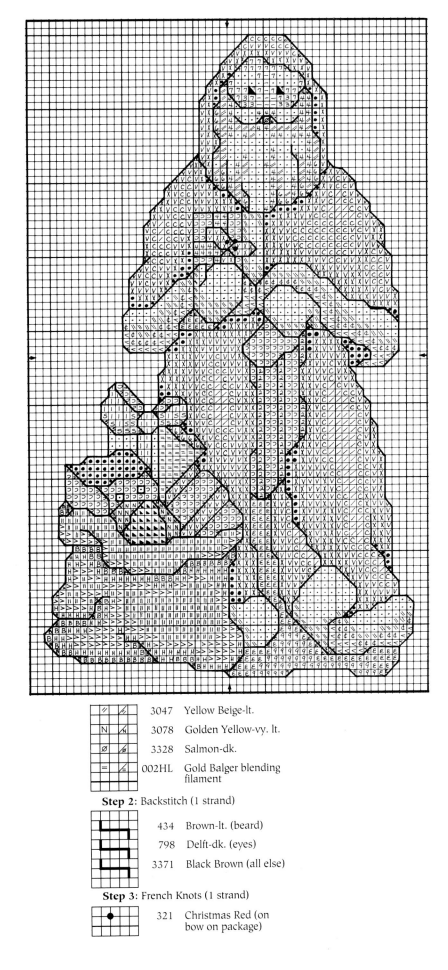

DMC Colors (used for sample)

Step 1: Cross-stitch (2 strands)

•	⁄		White
<	⁄	318	Steel Gray-lt.
I	⁄	321	Christmas Red
3	⁄	353	Peach
¢	⁄	415	Pearl Gray
B	⁄	433	Brown-med.
H	⁄	434	Brown-lt.
>	⁄	435	Brown-vy. lt.
‖	⁄	436	Tan
S	⁄	498	Christmas Red-dk.
●	⁄	500	Blue Green-vy. dk.
X	⁄	501	Blue Green-dk.
V	⁄	502	Blue Green
C	⁄	503	Blue Green-med.
⁄	⁄	504	Blue Green-lt.
Ɛ	⁄	738	Tan-vy. lt.
9	⁄	739	Tan-ultra vy. lt.
4	⁄	746	Off White
7	⁄	754	Peach-lt.
⑈	⁄	762	Pearl Gray-vy. lt.
◣	⁄	798	Delft-dk.
⊃	⁄	815	Garnet-med.
2	⁄	822	Beige Gray-lt.
−	⁄	948	Peach-vy. lt.
6	⁄	3046	Yellow Beige-med.

⁄	⁄	3047	Yellow Beige-lt.
N	⁄	3078	Golden Yellow-vy. lt.
ø	⁄	3328	Salmon-dk.
=	⁄	002HL	Gold Balger blending filament

Step 2: Backstitch (1 strand)

	434	Brown-lt. (beard)
	798	Delft-dk. (eyes)
	3371	Black Brown (all else)

Step 3: French Knots (1 strand)

●	321	Christmas Red (on bow on package)

97

Merry Christmas

SAMPLE

Sample in photograph was stitched on bisque 18-count Davosa over 2 threads. Design area is 22″ x 14⅜″. Fabric was cut 28″ x 21″.

FABRICS	DESIGN AREAS
11-count	18″ x 11¾″
14-count	14⅛″ x 9¼″
18-count	11″ x 7⅛″
22-count	9″ x 5⅞″

129
↑
└→198

DMC Colors
(used for sample)

Step 1: Cross-stitch (2 strands, except where noted)

4	4	433	Brown-med.
5	6	434	Brown-lt.
X	4	500	Blue Green-vy. dk. (*Note:* Inside letters, add 1 strand 009 emerald Balger blending filament.)
O	6	501	Blue Green-dk.
/	2	502	Blue Green
C	2	503	Blue Green-med.
^	4	725	Topaz (2 strands) + 002HL Gold Balger blending filament (1 strand)
3	3	726	Topaz-lt. (2 strands) + 002HL Gold Balger blending filament (1 strand)
7	1	727	Topaz-vy. lt. (2 strands) + 002HL Gold Balger blending filament (1 strand)
Z	2	781	Topaz-dk. (2 strands) + 002HL Gold Balger blending filament (1 strand)
V	2	782	Topaz-med. (2 strands) + 002HL Gold Balger blending filament (1 strand)
⊃	3	783	Christmas Gold (2 strands) + 002HL Gold Balger blending filament (1 strand)
1	/	814	Garnet-dk.
\	2	815	Garnet-med.
*	4	902	Garnet-vy. dk. (*Note:* For holly berries, add 1 strand 080HL garnet Balger blending filament.)

Step 2: Backstitch (1 strand)

	310 Black

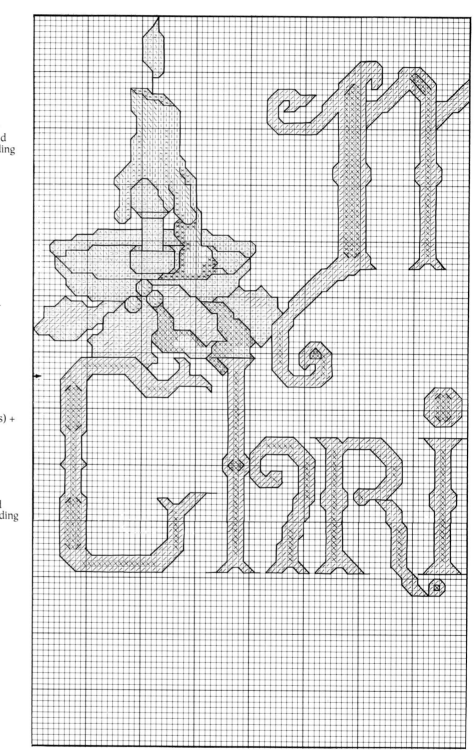

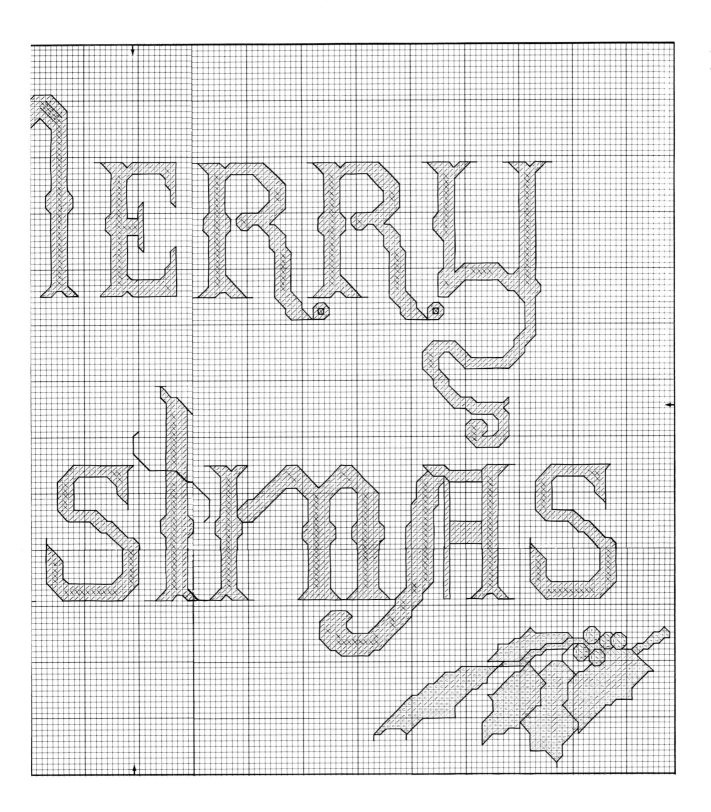

Country Kitchen

In our household, the center of activity is always the kitchen. We daily prove the truth of the old saying, "The kitchen is the heart of the home."

The ideal country kitchen, with its casual coziness, is perfectly suited to this role. It seems to welcome us, to invite us to sit a spell. Its familiar appointments—lace curtains, checked tablecloths, lovely collections of stoneware or willow baskets—are beautiful and useful. A cross-stitch sampler or two and windows opened to the outdoors' drowsy sounds add to the old-fashioned ambience.

Happily, this ideal place can really exist. For more ideas on making the kitchen the heart of your home, just turn the page. I had in mind just such a country kitchen when I created these cross-stitch designs.

Love Brings Us Together

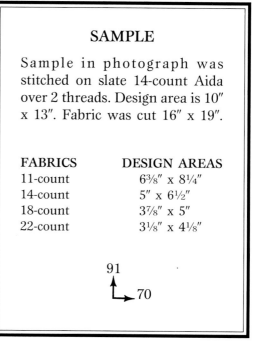

SAMPLE

Sample in photograph was stitched on slate 14-count Aida over 2 threads. Design area is 10″ x 13″. Fabric was cut 16″ x 19″.

FABRICS	DESIGN AREAS
11-count	6⅜″ x 8¼″
14-count	5″ x 6½″
18-count	3⅞″ x 5″
22-count	3⅛″ x 4⅛″

91
↑
└→70

INSTRUCTIONS

All seam allowances are ¼″.

1. With design centered, trim Aida to 12″ x 17″. From floral print, cut 1 (17″ x 22″) piece for backing; also cut 2 (12″ x 3″) strips and 2 (22″ x 3″) strips for border. From rose fabric, cut 1¼″-wide bias strips, piecing as needed to equal 62″. With bias strip and cording, make 62″ of corded piping.

2. With right sides facing and raw edges aligned, stitch piping around all edges of design piece. Use dressmakers' pen to mark center of 1 long edge of each border strip and center of each edge of design piece. With right sides facing, raw edges aligned, and center marks matching, sew short border strips to top and bottom of design piece and then long border strips to sides, sewing along stitching line of piping.

3. Stack fleece, top (right side up), and backing (right side down). Stitch, leaving an opening for turning. Trim corners and turn. Slipstitch opening closed.

4. Cut ribbon into 4 equal lengths and tie into bows. Tack 1 bow to piping at each corner.

MATERIALS

Completed cross-stitch on slate 14-count Aida; matching thread
½ yard (45″-wide) blue-and-rose floral print; matching thread
¼ yard (45″-wide) rose fabric; matching thread
1¾ yards of small cording
1 (17″ x 22″) piece of polyester fleece
1½ yards (¼″-wide) blue satin ribbon; matching thread
Dressmakers' pen

DMC Colors (used for sample)

Step 1: Cross-stitch (3 strands)

	White	504	Blue Green-lt.
221	Shell Pink-vy. dk.	535	Ash Gray-vy. lt.
223	Shell Pink-med.	738	Tan-vy. lt.
224	Shell Pink-lt.	739	Tan-ultra vy. lt.
225	Shell Pink-vy. lt.	744	Yellow-pale
310	Black	754	Peach-lt.
434	Brown-lt.	762	Pearl Gray-vy. lt.
435	Brown-vy. lt.	816	Garnet
437	Tan-lt.	822	Beige Gray-lt.
500	Blue Green-vy. dk.	827	Blue-vy. lt.
502	Blue Green	828	Blue-ultra vy. lt.
503	Blue Green-med.	840	Beige Brown-med.
		841	Beige Brown-lt.
		842	Beige Brown-vy. lt.

930	Antique Blue-dk.
931	Antique Blue-med.
932	Antique Blue-lt.
938	Coffee Brown-ultra dk.
948	Peach-vy. lt.
3022	Brown Gray-med.
3023	Brown Gray-lt.

Step 2: Backstitch (1 strand)

500 Blue Green-vy. dk. (lettering)
310 Black (all else)

Step 3: French Knots (1 strand)

310 Black

105

C Is for Cookies

SAMPLE

Sample in photograph was stitched on ash gray 14-count Aida over 2 threads. Design area is 11⅝" x 15¾". Fabric was cut 18" x 22".

FABRICS	DESIGN AREAS
11-count	7⅜" x 10"
14-count	5¾" x 7⅞"
18-count	4½" x 6⅛"
22-count	3⅝" x 5"

110
↑
└→ 81

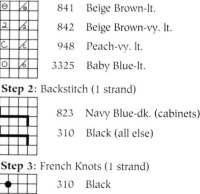

DMC Colors (used for sample)

Step 1: Cross-stitch (3 strands)

/	White
•	310 Black
*	312 Navy Blue-lt.
\\	318 Steel Gray-lt.
^	322 Navy Blue-vy. lt.
\\	334 Baby Blue-med.
Z	434 Brown-lt.
3	435 Brown-vy. lt.

–	436 Tan
I	437 Tan-lt.
+	498 Christmas Red-dk.
L	744 Yellow-pale
S	745 Yellow-lt. pale
X	754 Peach-lt.
V	762 Pearl Gray-vy. lt.
7	775 Baby Blue-vy. lt.
•	823 Navy Blue-dk.
/	840 Beige Brown-med.

Θ	841 Beige Brown-lt.
2	842 Beige Brown-vy. lt.
C	948 Peach-vy. lt.
O	3325 Baby Blue-lt.

Step 2: Backstitch (1 strand)

823 Navy Blue-dk. (cabinets)
310 Black (all else)

Step 3: French Knots (1 strand)
• 310 Black

Spice Bags

SAMPLES

Samples in photograph were stitched on ivory 28-count Jubilee over 2 threads. Design areas are: watermelon, 2⅛″ x 1⅞″; apples, 1⅝″ x 1½″; sifter, 2⅛″ x 1⅞″; and teapot, 2⅛″ x 1⅞″. Fabric was cut 9″ x 8″ for each.

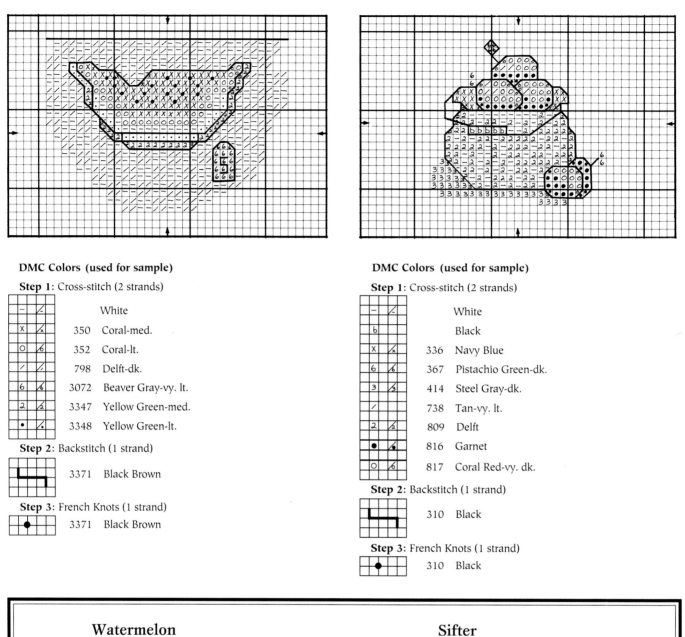

DMC Colors (used for sample)

Step 1: Cross-stitch (2 strands)

–	∕		White
X	∕x	350	Coral-med.
O	∕6	352	Coral-lt.
∕	∕	798	Delft-dk.
6	∕6	3072	Beaver Gray-vy. lt.
2	∕2	3347	Yellow Green-med.
•	∕•	3348	Yellow Green-lt.

Step 2: Backstitch (1 strand)

⌐	3371 Black Brown

Step 3: French Knots (1 strand)

•	3371 Black Brown

DMC Colors (used for sample)

Step 1: Cross-stitch (2 strands)

–	∕		White
b			Black
X	∕x	336	Navy Blue
6	∕6	367	Pistachio Green-dk.
3	∕3	414	Steel Gray-dk.
∕		738	Tan-vy. lt.
2	∕2	809	Delft
•	∕•	816	Garnet
O	∕6	817	Coral Red-vy. dk.

Step 2: Backstitch (1 strand)

⌐	310 Black

Step 3: French Knots (1 strand)

•	310 Black

Watermelon

FABRICS	DESIGN AREAS	
11-count	3″ x 2″	22
14-count	2¼″ x 1⅝″	
18-count	1¾″ x 1¼″	32
22-count	1½″ x 1″	

Apples

FABRICS	DESIGN AREAS	
11-count	2⅛″ x 1⅞″	21
14-count	1⅝″ x 1½″	
18-count	1¼″ x 1⅛″	23
22-count	1″ x 1″	

Sifter

FABRICS	DESIGN AREAS	
11-count	2⅝″ x 2⅜″	26
14-count	2⅛″ x 1⅞″	
18-count	1⅝″ x 1½″	29
22-count	1⅜″ x 1⅛″	

Teapot

FABRICS	DESIGN AREAS	
11-count	2¾″ x 2⅜″	26
14-count	2⅛″ x 1⅞″	
18-count	1⅝″ x 1½″	30
22-count	1⅜″ x 1⅛″	

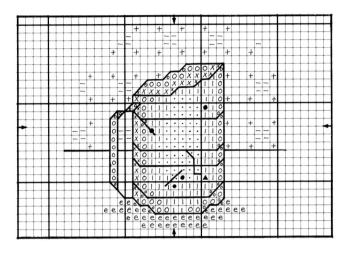

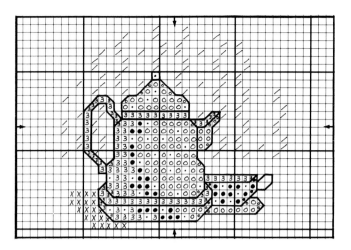

DMC Colors (used for sample)

Step 1: Cross-stitch (2 strands)

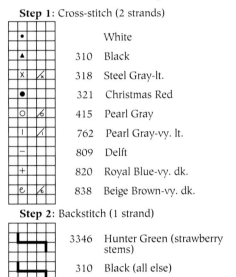

•		White
▲		310 Black
X	╱	318 Steel Gray-lt.
●		321 Christmas Red
O	╱	415 Pearl Gray
I	╱	762 Pearl Gray-vy. lt.
–		809 Delft
+		820 Royal Blue-vy. dk.
e	╱	838 Beige Brown-vy. dk.

Step 2: Backstitch (1 strand)

⌐_	3346 Hunter Green (strawberry stems)
⌐_	310 Black (all else)

DMC Colors (used for sample)

Step 1: Cross-stitch (2 strands)

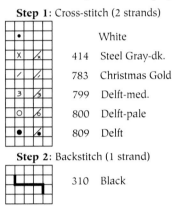

•		White
X	╱	414 Steel Gray-dk.
╱	╱	783 Christmas Gold
3	╱	799 Delft-med.
O	╱	800 Delft-pale
●	╱	809 Delft

Step 2: Backstitch (1 strand)

⌐_	310 Black

MATERIALS (for 1 spice bag)

Completed cross-stitch on ivory 28-count Jubilee; matching thread
1 (5″) square of ivory 28-count Jubilee for back
¼ yard (³⁄₈″-wide) red or blue ribbon; matching thread
Spice-scented potpourri

INSTRUCTIONS

All seam allowances are ¾″.

1. With design centered, trim design piece to a 5″ square.

2. With wrong sides facing and raw edges aligned, stitch design piece to back, leaving an opening on 1 side. Stuff moderately with potpourri. Stitch opening closed with tiny running stitches.

3. To fringe seam allowance, begin at raw edge on 1 side of bag and pull all lengthwise threads up to seamline. Repeat for remaining sides.

4. Tie ribbon into a bow and tack to 1 upper corner of sachet.

Kitchen Sampler

SAMPLE

Sample in photograph was stitched on natural brown undyed 26-count linen over 2 threads. Design area is 7" x 7⅞". Fabric was cut 13" x 14".

FABRICS	DESIGN AREAS
11-count	8⅛" x 9¼"
14-count	6⅜" x 7¼"
18-count	5" x 5⅝"
22-count	4⅛" x 4⅝"

102
→ 90

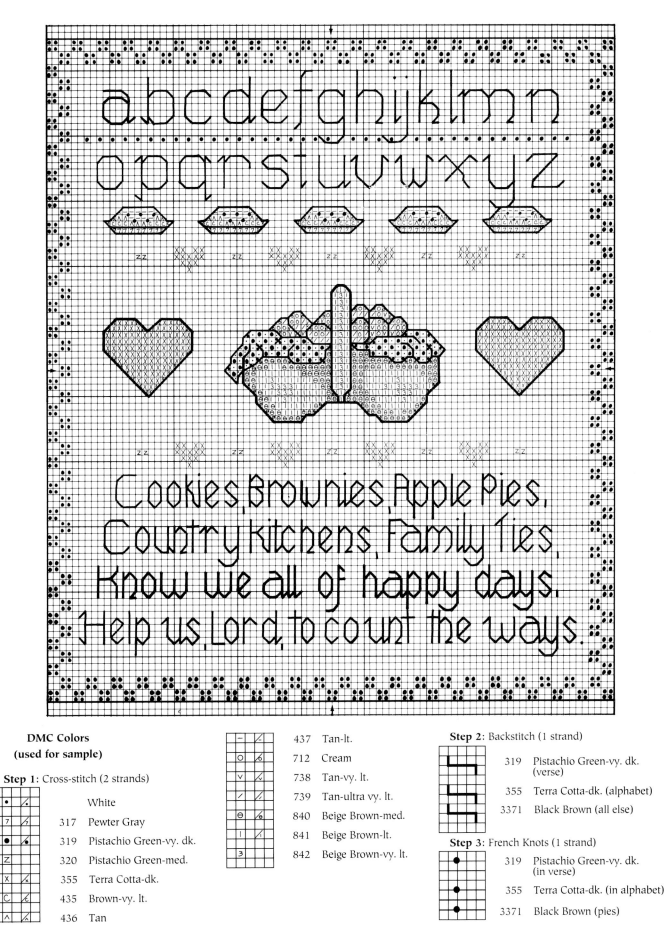

DMC Colors
(used for sample)

Step 1: Cross-stitch (2 strands)

•	∕
7	7
●	∕
Z	
X	∕
C	∕
∧	∕

White
317   Pewter Gray
319   Pistachio Green-vy. dk.
320   Pistachio Green-med.
355   Terra Cotta-dk.
435   Brown-vy. lt.
436   Tan

−	∕
O	6
V	∕
∕	∕
θ	6
I	∕
3	

437   Tan-lt.
712   Cream
738   Tan-vy. lt.
739   Tan-ultra vy. lt.
840   Beige Brown-med.
841   Beige Brown-lt.
842   Beige Brown-vy. lt.

Step 2: Backstitch (1 strand)

319   Pistachio Green-vy. dk. (verse)
355   Terra Cotta-dk. (alphabet)
3371   Black Brown (all else)

Step 3: French Knots (1 strand)

319   Pistachio Green-vy. dk. (in verse)
355   Terra Cotta-dk. (in alphabet)
3371   Black Brown (pies)

Bless My Country Kitchen

SAMPLES

Samples in photograph were stitched on parchment 14-count Terry Towel over 1 thread and on parchment 14-count Pot Holder over 1 thread. Design area is 5⅝" x 2⅜" for towel, 7¼" x 2⅜" for pot holder (with top and bottom borders extended as indicated below).

For terry towel, center design in Aida area, leaving 3 threads unworked above and below design and 62 threads unworked on each side. For pot holder, center design in Aida area, leaving 21 threads unworked above and below design; extend top and bottom borders of design 12 stitches on each side to meet sides of pot holder.

FABRICS	DESIGN AREAS
11-count	7⅛" x 3⅛"
18-count	4⅜" x 1⅞"
22-count	3½" x 1½"

34

78

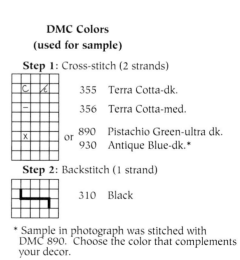

DMC Colors
(used for sample)

Step 1: Cross-stitch (2 strands)

C	∠	355 Terra Cotta-dk.
−		356 Terra Cotta-med.
X		or 890 Pistachio Green-ultra dk.
		930 Antique Blue-dk.*

Step 2: Backstitch (1 strand)

310   Black

* Sample in photograph was stitched with DMC 890. Choose the color that complements your decor.

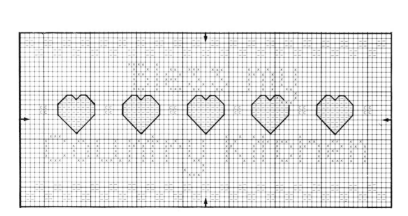

Country Days

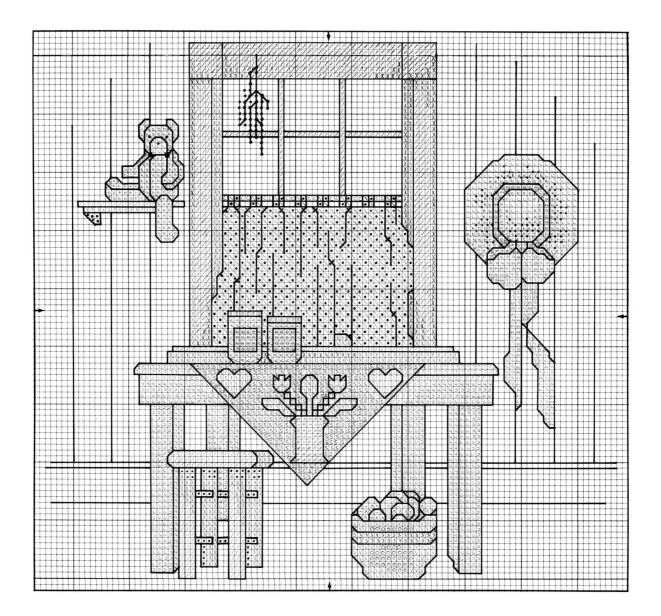

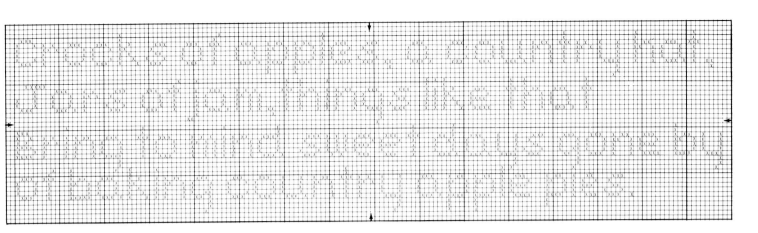

DMC Colors
(used for sample)

Step 1: Cross-stitch (2 strands)

\	X		Ecru
I	/	221	Shell Pink-vy. dk.
2	Z	223	Shell Pink-med.
S	S	225	Shell Pink-vy. lt.
3	Z	312	Navy Blue-lt.
8	Z	318	Steel Gray-lt.
−	Z	321	Christmas Red
C	Z	433	Brown-med.
4	Z	434	Brown-lt.
ↄ	Z	435	Brown-vy. lt.
6	Z	436	Tan
7	Z	437	Tan-lt.
<	Z	597	Turquoise
V	Z	642	Beige Gray-dk.
O	Z	644	Beige Gray-med.
K	Z	676	Old Gold-lt.
L	Z	677	Old Gold-vy. lt.
e	Z	680	Old Gold-dk.
b	Z	729	Old Gold-med.
Z	Z	814	Garnet-dk.
^	Z	816	Garnet
>	Z	924	Slate Green-vy. dk.
9	Z	926	Slate Green
θ	Z	927	Slate Green-med.
\\	Z	928	Slate Green-lt.
•	Z	930	Antique Blue-dk.
X	x	931	Antique Blue-med.
/	Z	932	Antique Blue-lt.
//	Z	3047	Yellow Beige-lt.

Step 2: Backstitch (1 strand, except where noted)

930 Antique Blue-dk. (2 strands) (baseboards)

3046 Yellow Beige-med. (2 strands) (walls)

3051 Green Gray-dk. (sage)

3371 Black Brown (bear, shelf, hat)

310 Black (all else)

Step 3: French Knots (1 strand)

● 310 Black (bear's eyes and nose)

● 3041 Antique Violet-med. (flowers on hat on wall and spray in window)*

● 3052 Green Gray-med. (flowers on hat on wall and spray in window)*

Step 4: Bow (6 strands)

■ ■ 223 Shell Pink-med. (Thread floss in and out at marked points and tie in bow.)

* Alternate colors as desired.

All-American Country

My husband, Scoot, and I are proud patriots. Both of our fathers served in the armed forces, and for 10 years Scoot was a pilot in the U.S. Air Force.

Perhaps it's not surprising, therefore, that we have a passion for Americana. Displayed throughout our home are pieces from our collection and symbols of our family's service to our country. It's an eclectic mix that includes more than a few of my cross-stitch samplers, but I value most my father's World War II medals, which are given the place of honor.

I hope you, too, will allow your star-spangled spirit to soar with my Americana designs, which all feature plenty of the red, white, and blue.

Land of My Birth

★ ★

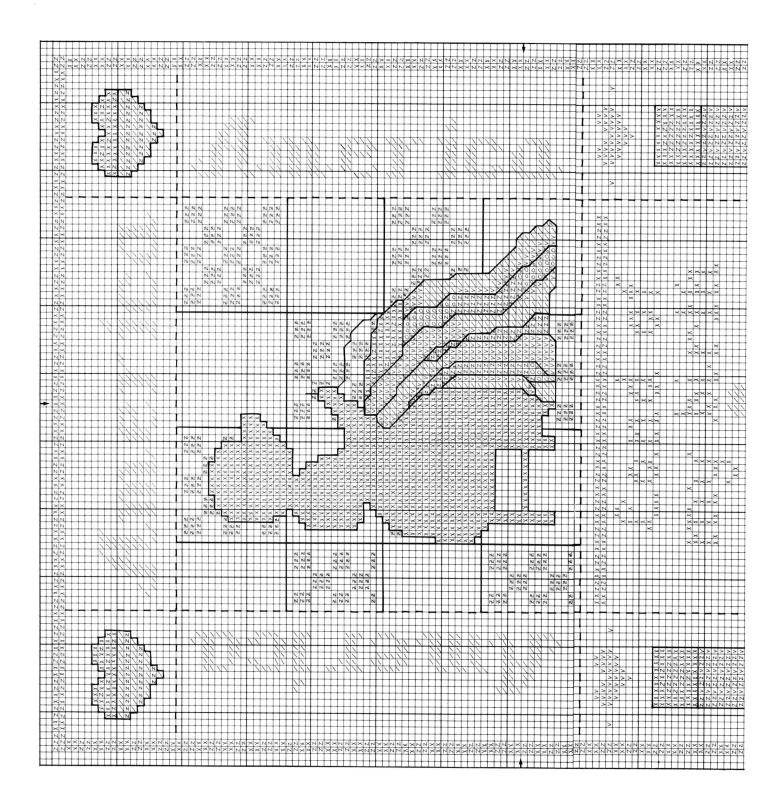

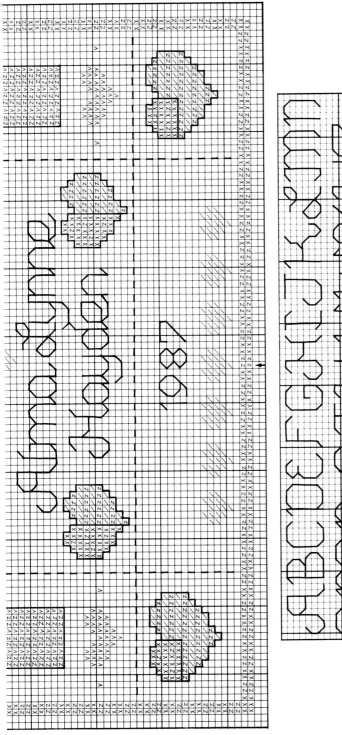

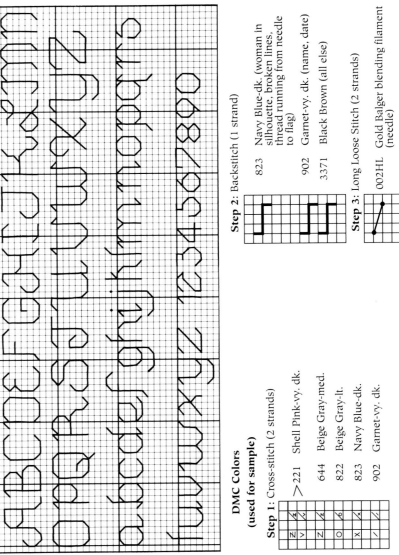

Step 2: Backstitch (1 strand)

823 Navy Blue-dk. (woman in silhouette, broken lines, thread running from needle to flag)

902 Garnet-vy. dk. (name, date)

3371 Black Brown (all else)

Step 3: Long Loose Stitch (2 strands)

002HL Gold Balger blending filament (needle)

DMC Colors
(used for sample)

Step 1: Cross-stitch (2 strands)

N	N	221	Shell Pink-vy. dk.
>	>	644	Beige Gray-med.
Z	Z	822	Beige Gray-lt.
O	6	823	Navy Blue-dk.
X	X	902	Garnet-vy. dk.
/	/		

All-American Welcome

★ ★

SAMPLE

Sample in photograph was stitched on khaki 18-count Davosa over 2 threads. Design area is 17⅜″ x 9½″. Fabric was cut 24″ x 16″.

FABRICS	DESIGN AREAS
11-count	14⅛″ x 7⅞″
14-count	11⅛″ x 6⅛″
18-count	8⅝″ x 4¾″
22-count	7⅛″ x 3⅞″

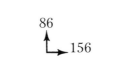

86
↑
└→156

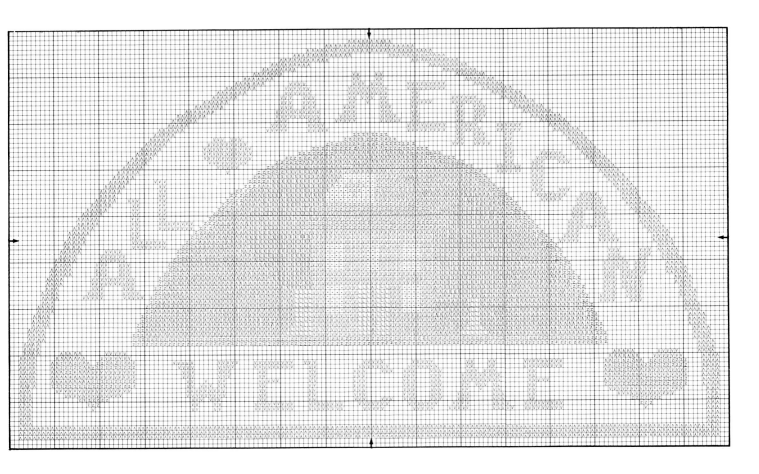

MATERIALS

Completed cross-stitch on khaki 18-count Davosa; matching thread
½ yard (45″-wide) blue-and-red plaid; matching thread
1½ yards of medium cording
Stuffing

INSTRUCTIONS

All seam allowances are ¼″.

1. Trim design piece 1″ outside stitched design. From plaid, cut 1 piece to match design piece for pillow back; also cut 1½″-wide bias strips, piecing as needed to equal 54″. With bias strip and cording, make 54″ of corded piping.

2. With right sides facing and raw edges aligned, stitch piping around all edges of pillow front.

3. With right sides facing and raw edges aligned, stitch pillow front to back, sewing along stitching line of piping and leaving an opening on straight edge for turning. Clip curves, trim corners, and turn. Stuff firmly. Slipstitch opening closed.

DMC Colors
(used for sample)

Step 1: Cross-stitch (3 strands)

v	221	Shell Pink-vy. dk.
•	336	Navy Blue
x	501	Blue Green-dk.
z	822	Beige Gray-lt.
^	823	Navy Blue-dk.
L	841	Beige Brown-lt.

Liberty Land

★ ★

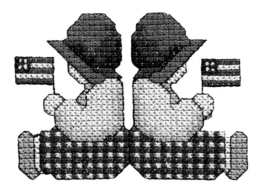

Framed Piece

FABRICS	DESIGN AREAS
11-count	4¾" x 17⅝"
14-count	3¾" x 13⅞"
18-count	3" x 10¾"
22-count	2⅜" x 8⅞"

194

53

Pillow with Letters

FABRICS	DESIGN AREAS
11-count	4¾" x 5⅞"
14-count	3¾" x 4⅝"
18-count	3" x 3⅝"
22-count	2⅜" x 3"

65
53

Pillow with Numbers

FABRICS	DESIGN AREAS
11-count	4" x 4¾"
14-count	3⅛" x 3¾"
18-count	2⅜" x 3"
22-count	2" x 2⅜"

53
43

MATERIALS (for 1 pillow)

Completed cross-stitch on khaki 27-count Linda; matching thread
½ yard (45"-wide) coordinating fabric; matching thread
¼ yard (45"-wide) contrasting fabric; matching thread
1⅛ yards of medium cording
Dressmakers' pen
Stuffing

INSTRUCTIONS

All seam allowances are ¼".

1. With design centered, trim Linda to 5½" x 6½". From coordinating fabric, cut 1 (8½" x 9½") piece for back; also cut 2 (6½" x 2") strips and 2 (8½" x 2") strips for border and 3 (30" x 6") strips for ruffle. From contrasting fabric, cut 1½"-wide bias strips, piecing as needed to equal 40". With bias strip and cording, make 40" of corded piping.

2. To make pillow front: Use dressmakers' pen to mark center of 1 long edge of each border strip and center of each edge of design piece. With right sides facing, raw edges aligned, and center marks matching, sew short border strips to sides of design piece and then long border strips to top and bottom.

3. With right sides facing and raw edges aligned, pin piping around all edges of pillow front. Baste piping in place.

4. To make ruffle: With right sides facing and raw edges aligned, stitch ends of 3 ruffle strips together to make 1 (89" x 6") strip. Press seams open. With right sides facing and raw edges aligned, fold strip in half lengthwise to measure 3" wide; stitch ends. Turn and press. Run gathering threads along long raw edges through both layers. Mark ruffle at 21", 44", and 65". Beginning at bottom left-hand corner, pin ruffle to right side of pillow front, aligning raw edges and placing marks at corners. Gather ruffle to fit. Stitch along stitching line of piping, through all layers.

5. Place pillow back over front, with right sides facing, raw edges aligned, and piping and ruffle toward center. Stitch, leaving an opening on 1 side. Trim corners and turn. Stuff firmly. Slip-stitch opening closed.

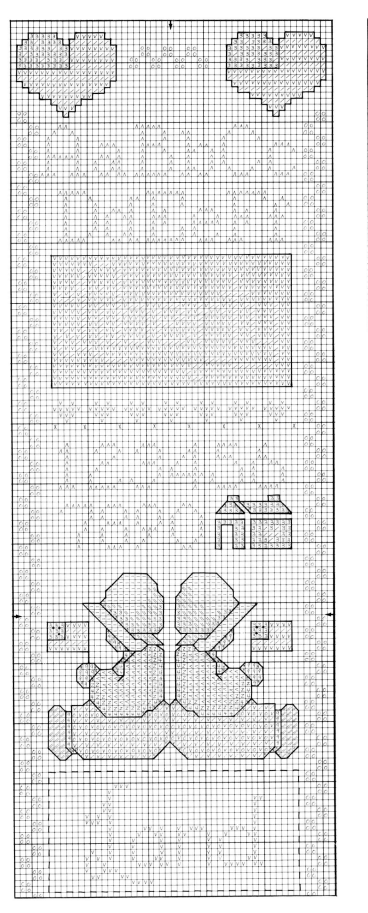

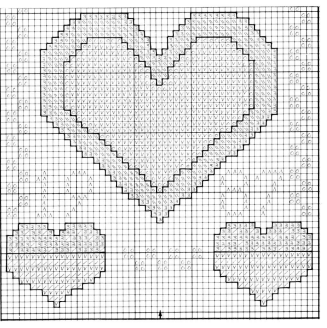

DMC Colors
(used for sample)

Step 2: Backstitch (1 strand)

⌐	3033 Mocha Brown-vy. lt. (broken lines)
⌐	3371 Black Brown (all else)

Step 3: French Knots (1 strand)

●	3033 Mocha Brown-vy. lt.

129

Two for the
Red, White, and Blue

★ ★

SAMPLES

Samples in photograph were stitched on khaki 14-count Aida over 1 thread. Design areas are 2¾″ x 2¾″ for angel, 2¼″ x 2½″ for tulip. Fabric was cut 9″ x 9″ for each.

Angel

FABRICS	DESIGN AREAS
11-count	3½″ x 3½″
18-count	2⅛″ x 2⅛″
22-count	1¾″ x 1¾″

39
↑
→ 38

Tulip

FABRICS	DESIGN AREAS
11-count	2⅞″ x 3⅛″
18-count	1¾″ x 2″
22-count	1⅜″ x 1⅝″

35
↑
→ 31

DMC Colors
(used for sample)

Step 1: Cross-stitch (2 strands)

		221	Shell Pink-vy. dk.
O		336	Navy Blue
		437	Tan-lt.
V		642	Beige Gray-dk.
/		644	Beige Gray-med.
–		738	Tan-vy. lt.
7		754	Peach-lt.
X		823	Navy Blue-dk.
Z		902	Garnet-vy. dk.

Step 2: Backstitch (1 strand)

		3371	Black Brown

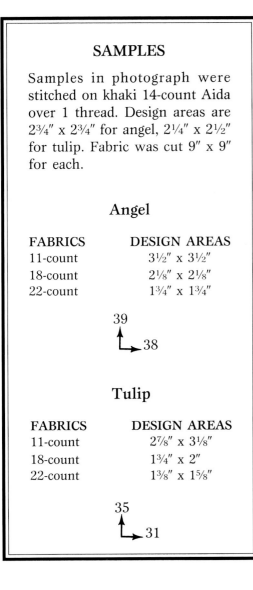

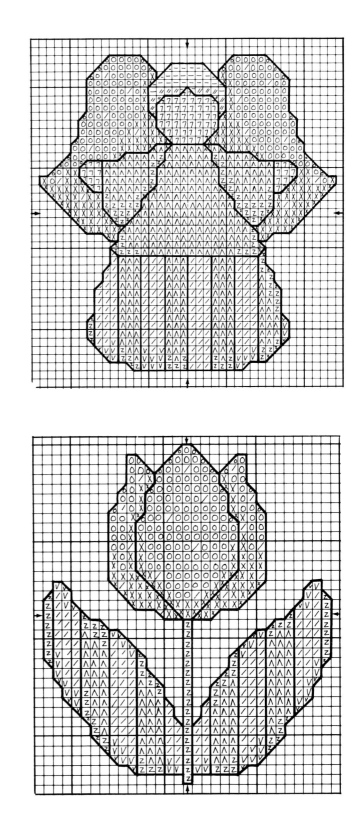

Priscilla Frances Whitehanky

★ ★

SAMPLE

Sample in photograph was stitched on parchment 14-count Yorkshire Aida over 1 thread. Design area is 6″ x 9½″. Fabric was cut 18″ x 18″. (*Note:* For a framed piece, cut fabric 12″ x 16″.)

FABRICS	DESIGN AREAS
11-count	7⅝″ x 12⅛″
18-count	4⅝″ x 7⅜″
22-count	3⅞″ x 6″

133

↱ 84

MATERIALS

Completed cross-stitch on parchment 14-count Yorkshire Aida

Purchased (12″-diameter, 7″-deep) bandbox

1 yard (45″-wide) red-and-white-striped cotton fabric with 1″ stripes

¼ yard (45″-wide) navy-and-white-star cotton fabric

⅛ yard (45″-wide) navy fabric; matching thread

1 (12″) square of polyester fleece

1 yard of fusible interfacing

1⅛ yards (1⅞″-wide) ivory/burgundy 14-count Aida prefinished ribbon

16 tea bags

Hot-glue gun and glue sticks

INSTRUCTIONS

All seam allowances are ¼″.

1. To tea-dye cotton fabric: Steep tea bags in a half-gallon of very hot water for 20 minutes. Remove tea bags. Soak fabric in tea, checking every 5 minutes for depth of color. (*Note:* Fabric, when dry, will be lighter than it appears when wet.) When fabric is just a little darker than desired (this usually takes between 10 and 35 minutes), remove fabric, squeeze out water, and dry in a clothes dryer with an old terry-cloth towel to absorb tea residue. Press to set color.

2. With design centered, trim Yorkshire Aida to 1 (15″) circle. From tea-dyed red-and-white-striped fabric, cut 1 (40″ x 10″) strip, 1 (40″ x 8″) strip, and 1 (40″ x 4″) strip. Place bandbox on remaining red-and-white-striped fabric, trace around it, and cut out circle; repeat to cut out another circle. From tea-dyed navy-and-white-star fabric, cut 1 (9″ x 6″) rectangle. From navy fabric, cut 1 (36″ x 4½″) strip. From square of fleece, cut 1 (12″) circle.

3. For each tea-dyed fabric piece cut in Step 2, cut a piece of fusible interfacing to match. Iron interfacing pieces to wrong sides of matching fabric pieces.

4. To finish outside of box: Center, wrap, and glue 40″ x 10″ fabric strip around box sides, smoothing fabric as you go and overlapping ends. Smooth, ease, and glue top edge of strip to inside of box and bottom edge of strip to bottom of box. Smooth and glue navy-and-white-star rectangle on box side where desired, folding and gluing top edge inside box. Center and glue 1 fabric circle on box bottom.

5. To finish inside: Smooth and glue 40″ x 8″ strip around inside of box, with 1 long edge aligned with top of box. Smooth, ease, and glue excess fabric to bottom. Center and glue remaining fabric circle on bottom, covering excess.

6. To finish lid: Center fleece circle on lid and glue in place. Center design piece on fleece and glue edges of design piece to lid rim, clipping if necessary. Fold ½″ along 1 long edge of 40″ x 4″ strip to wrong side; press. With folded edge of strip aligned with top edge of lid, glue strip around rim. Fold and glue excess fabric to inside

of rim. With edge of Aida ribbon at top of rim, glue ribbon around rim.

7. To make bow: With right sides facing and raw edges aligned, fold navy fabric strip in half lengthwise. Stitch together raw edges along long side and 1 end; turn through open end. Fold raw edge ½″ to inside of open end; slipstitch opening closed. Press. Tie strip into a bow; glue bow to rim of lid (see photo for placement).

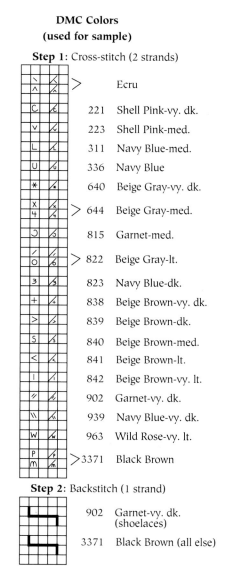

DMC Colors
(used for sample)

Step 1: Cross-stitch (2 strands)

	>		Ecru
		221	Shell Pink-vy. dk.
		223	Shell Pink-med.
		311	Navy Blue-med.
		336	Navy Blue
		640	Beige Gray-vy. dk.
	>	644	Beige Gray-med.
		815	Garnet-med.
	>	822	Beige Gray-lt.
		823	Navy Blue-dk.
		838	Beige Brown-vy. dk.
		839	Beige Brown-dk.
		840	Beige Brown-med.
		841	Beige Brown-lt.
		842	Beige Brown-vy. lt.
		902	Garnet-vy. dk.
		939	Navy Blue-vy. dk.
		963	Wild Rose-vy. lt.
	>	3371	Black Brown

Step 2: Backstitch (1 strand)

902	Garnet-vy. dk. (shoelaces)
3371	Black Brown (all else)

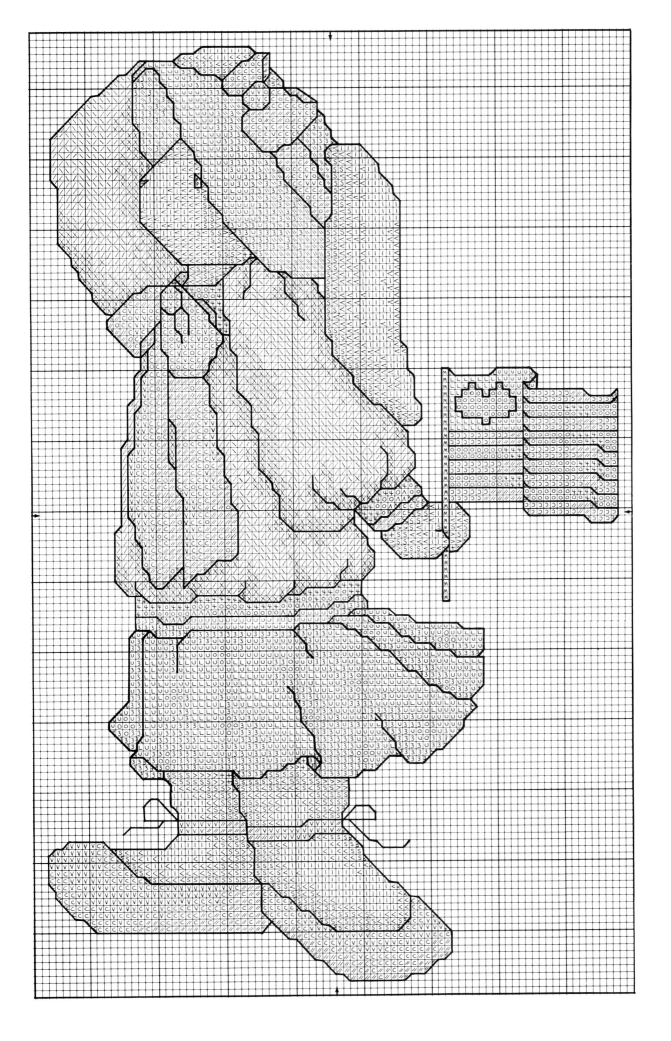

I Love America

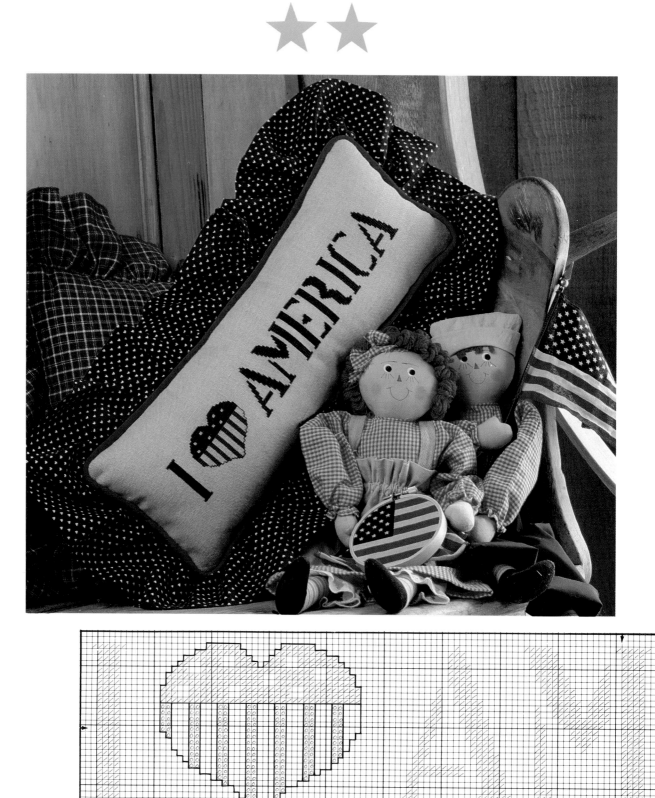

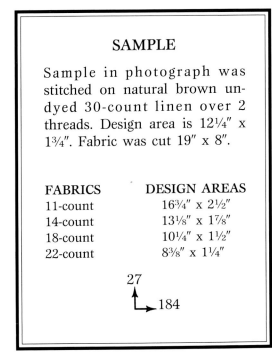
MATERIALS

Completed cross-stitch on natural brown undyed 30-count linen; matching thread
¼ yard (45″-wide) maroon fabric; matching thread
½ yard (45″-wide) navy miniprint; matching thread
1⅜ yards of medium cording
Dressmakers' pen
Stuffing

INSTRUCTIONS

All seam allowances are ¼″.

1. With design centered, trim linen to 16¾″ x 6¼″. From maroon fabric, cut 1 (16¾″ x 6¼″) piece for pillow back; also cut 1½″-wide bias strips, piecing as needed to equal 50″. From mini-print, cut 3 (39″ x 6″) strips for ruffle. With bias strip and cording, make 50″ of corded piping.

2. With right sides facing and raw edges aligned, pin piping around all edges of pillow front. Baste piping in place.

3. To make ruffle: With right sides facing and raw edges aligned, stitch ends of 3 miniprint strips together to make 1 (116″ x 6″) strip. Press seams open. With right sides facing and raw edges aligned, fold strip in half lengthwise to measure 3″ wide; stitch ends. Turn and press. Run gathering threads along raw edges through both layers. Mark ruffle at 42″, 58″, and 100″. Beginning at bottom left-hand corner, pin ruffle to right side of pillow front, aligning raw edges and placing marks at corners. Gather ruffle to fit. Stitch along stitching line of piping, through all layers.

4. Place pillow back over front, with right sides facing, raw edges aligned, and piping and ruffle toward center. Stitch, leaving an opening on 1 side. Trim corners and turn. Stuff firmly. Slip-stitch opening closed.

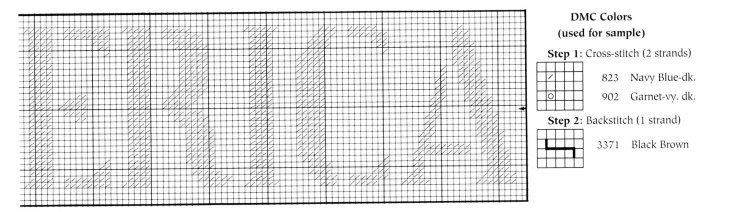

DMC Colors
(used for sample)

Step 1: Cross-stitch (2 strands)

/				823 Navy Blue-dk.
o				902 Garnet-vy. dk.

Step 2: Backstitch (1 strand)

3371 Black Brown

Liberty Bunnies

★ ★

SAMPLE

Sample in photograph was stitched on wedgewood 25-count Lugana over 2 threads. Design area is 11″ x 8⅞″. Fabric was cut 17″ x 15″.

FABRICS	DESIGN AREAS
11-count	12½″ x 10⅛″
14-count	9⅞″ x 7⅞″
18-count	7⅝″ x 6⅛″
22-count	6¼″ x 5″

111
⤴︎ ⤵︎138

MATERIALS

Completed cross-stitch on wedgewood 25-count Lugana; matching thread
1 yard (45″-wide) maroon miniprint; matching thread
¼ yard (45″-wide) navy fabric; matching thread
1⅝ yards of medium cording
Dressmakers' pen
Stuffing

INSTRUCTIONS

All seam allowances are ¼″.

1. With design centered, trim Lugana to 14½″ x 12½″. From maroon miniprint, cut 1 (14½″ x 12½″) piece for pillow back and 3 (45″ x 7″) strips for ruffle. From navy fabric, cut 1½″-wide bias strips, piecing as needed to equal 58″. With bias strip and cording, make 58″ of corded piping.

2. With right sides facing and raw edges aligned, pin piping around all edges of pillow front. Baste piping in place.

3. With right sides facing and raw edges aligned, stitch ends of 3 maroon miniprint strips together to make 1 (134″ x 7″) strip. Press seams open. With right sides facing and raw edges aligned, fold strip in half lengthwise to measure 3½″ wide; stitch ends. Turn; press. Run gathering threads along raw edges through both layers. Mark ruffle at 36″, 67″, and 103″. Beginning at bottom left-hand corner, pin ruffle to right side of pillow front, aligning raw edges and placing marks at corners. Gather ruffle to fit. Stitch along stitching line of piping, through all layers.

4. With right sides facing, raw edges aligned, and piping and ruffle toward center, stitch pillow front to back, leaving an opening on 1 side. Trim corners; turn and stuff. Slipstitch opening closed.

DMC Colors (used for sample)

Step 1: Cross-stitch (2 strands)

+	⁄	221	Shell Pink-vy. dk.
ε	⁄	223	Shell Pink-med.
‖	⁄	311	Navy Blue-med.
l	⁄	312	Navy Blue-lt.
7	⁄	317	Pewter Gray
−	⁄	318	Steel Gray-lt.
>	⁄	336	Navy Blue
4	⁄	413	Pewter Gray-dk.
∧	⁄	414	Steel Gray-dk.
•	⁄	415	Pearl Gray
N	⁄	498	Christmas Red-dk.
6	⁄	642	Beige Gray-dk.
<	⁄	644	Beige Gray-med.
Z	⁄	758	Terra Cotta-lt.
=	⁄	815	Garnet-med.
O	⁄	822	Beige Gray-lt.
8	⁄	823	Navy Blue-dk.
*	⁄	838	Beige Brown-vy. dk.
9	⁄	839	Beige Brown-dk.
X	⁄	840	Beige Brown-med.
V	⁄	841	Beige Brown-lt.
⁄	⁄	842	Beige Brown-vy. lt.
e	⁄	844	Beaver Gray-ultra dk.
∅	⁄	902	Garnet-vy. dk.
3	⁄	930	Antique Blue-dk.
∽	⁄	931	Antique Blue-med.
⊂	⁄	932	Antique Blue-lt.
■		3371	Black Brown

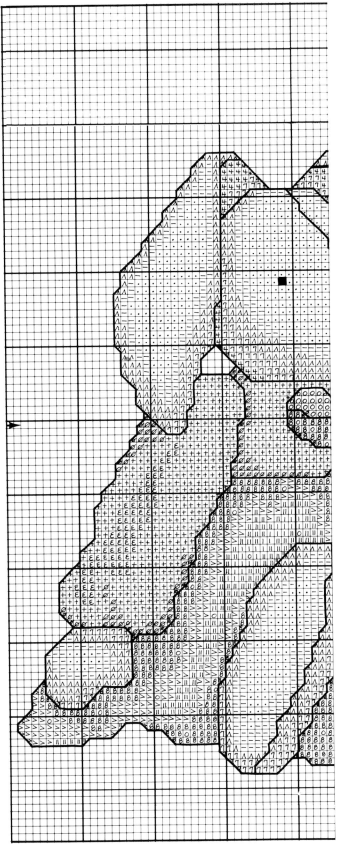

Step 2: Backstitch (1 strand)

3371   Black Brown

General Instructions

Preparation

Design Area. To determine design area of a design stitched over one thread, divide stitch count of design by thread count of fabric. If design is stitched over two threads, divide stitch count by one-half of thread count. In designations of design areas, horizontal measurements are given first, vertical measurements second.

Fabrics. Most of the designs in this book were stitched on even-weave fabrics made especially for cross-stitch. In the sample paragraphs, fabrics are identified by color, thread count, and name. If your local needlework shop does not stock a particular fabric, see Suppliers for information on ordering it.

Floss. The designs in this book call for DMC six-strand embroidery floss. (A few designs also use Balger metallic threads.) Cut floss into 18″ lengths; separate strands; then recombine and thread needle with number of strands called for in color codes.

Graphs and Color Codes. In graphs, a square containing a symbol represents one stitch to be worked on fabric. Each symbol corresponds to a specific color of DMC floss, identified by number and name in color code. Stitches other than cross-stitch, such as backstitch and French knots, are also represented in both graphs and color codes.

Stitch Count. Stitch count equals number of stitches in design, counted both horizontally and vertically, as indicated by arrows whose bases are joined in a right angle.

Thread Count. Thread count equals number of parallel threads per inch in weave of fabric. Thus 14-count fabric has 14 threads per inch, 18-count fabric has 18 threads per inch, and so on.

Getting Started

Hoop or Frame. Using an embroidery hoop or frame to keep fabric taut makes it easier to form uniform stitches. Select a hoop or frame large enough to accommodate entire design. Place screw or clamp of hoop in a 10 o'clock position (or 2 o'clock, if you are left-handed) to keep it from catching floss.

Needles. To avoid splitting fabric threads, use a blunt tapestry needle. With fabric that has 11 or fewer threads per inch, use a size-24 needle. With fabric that has 14 threads per inch, use a size-24 or 26 needle. With fabric that has 16 or more threads per inch, use a size-26 needle.

Preparing Fabric. Cut fabric *at least* 3″ larger on all sides than design area. To keep edges of fabric from fraying while you work on design, whipstitch or machine-zigzag raw edges or apply liquid ravel preventer and allow to dry.

Centering Design. To make sure that design, when completed, is centered on fabric, use the following procedure. First, fold fabric into quarters, folding from left to right and then from top to bottom. Where folds intersect is center of fabric. To find center of design, follow lines indicated by arrows at edges of graph until lines intersect. If there is a symbol at center of design, begin stitching there. If there is no symbol at center of design, calculate distance from center of design to nearest symbol and begin stitching there.

Securing Floss. Bring needle and most of floss *up* through fabric, holding a 1″ tail of floss behind fabric where first stitches will be taken. Work first four or five stitches over tail of floss to secure it.

You can also use the waste knot. After tying a knot at end of floss, bring needle *down* through fabric about 1″ from where first stitch will be taken. Plan placement of waste knot so that first four or five stitches will cover and secure 1″ of floss on back of fabric, as described above. After floss has been secured, cut off knot.

To secure floss when finished, run needle and floss under four or five stitches on back of design and trim tail close. Subsequent lengths of floss may be secured in the same manner.

Working the Design

Keeping Design Clean. Always wash your hands well and avoid using hand creams and lotions before you begin stitching. As each section is stitched, fold or roll fabric so that front of embroidery faces inward.

Working over One Fabric Thread. For smooth, even stitches, use the push-and-pull method when working over one thread. Push needle straight up through fabric and pull floss completely through to front of fabric. To bring needle to back again, push needle straight down and pull needle and floss completely through to back.

Working over Two Fabric Threads. Some experts recommend using the push-and-pull method (see above) for working over either one or two threads, while others recommend using the sewing method for working over two threads. To use the sewing method, first push needle straight up through fabric at 1. Then insert needle at 2 from front of fabric. Guide tip of needle to back of fabric and then to front at 3 in one motion; pull needle and floss through fabric, keeping your stitching hand in front of fabric at all times (Diagram A).

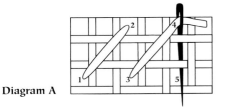

Diagram A

Carrying Floss. To carry floss, weave it under previously worked stitches on the back. Never carry floss across fabric that is not or will not be stitched. Carried threads, especially dark ones, will show through open fabric.

Untwisting Floss. Floss covers best when lying flat against fabric. If floss becomes twisted, drop your needle and allow floss to unwind itself. Cut floss no longer than 18″, because longer lengths tend to twist and knot during stitching.

Finishing Up

Signing and Dating the Work. Always sign and date your work to enrich its meaning for future generations. Using a neutral color of floss, back-stitch or cross-stitch your name or initials and the year in the lower right-hand corner.

Setting Colors. Be sure there are no stains in fabric, since treatment will set stains as well as colors. (Spot-clean any stains with soap and water.) Set colors of floss by soaking work for approximately 10 minutes in 1 quart of cool water to which you have added ½ cup of white vinegar. Rinse thoroughly.

Cleaning the Work. Soak work in cool water with a mild soap for about 10 minutes. Rinse thoroughly. Roll work in a towel to remove excess water; do not wring. Place face down on a dry towel and, with iron on warm setting, iron until dry.

Stitches

Cross-Stitch. When a symbol takes up an entire square on the graph, make one complete cross-stitch. Bring needle and thread up at 1, down at 2, up at 3, and down again at 4 (Diagram B).

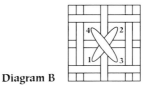

Diagram B

For horizontal rows, work understitches in one journey, moving from left to right; then work over-stitches in a second journey, moving from right to left (Diagram C). For vertical rows, complete each stitch individually (Diagram D). All stitches should lie in the same direction—that is, all understitches must slant in the same direction and all overstitches must slant in the opposite direction.

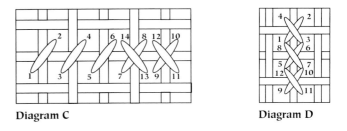

Diagram C   Diagram D

When a symbol fills only half of a square on the graph, make a three-quarter stitch (Diagram E). (This creates a curved line in design.) If you are working over one thread, the short understitch will pierce the fabric thread; if you are working over two threads, it will go down in the hole between the two threads. In each case the long stitch is the over-stitch, even though this may violate the rule that all stitches should lie in the same direction.

When two symbols occupy a single square on the graph, make a three-quarter stitch and a quarter stitch to fill the square. Which symbol takes which stitch depends on the line you want to emphasize—use the three-quarter stitch to articulate the dominant line or color (Diagram F).

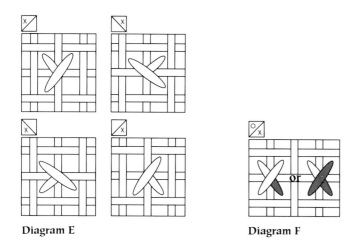

Diagram E　　　　　　　**Diagram F**

Half-cross. Sometimes part of a design calls for only the first half, or the understitch, of a cross-stitch to be worked. Called a half-cross, this stitch is represented by its own symbol and step in the color code (Diagram G).

Smyrna Cross. Working over two threads, make one cross-stitch and then another one over it (Diagram H).

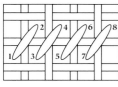

Diagram G　　　　　　　**Diagram H**

Backstitch. Bring needle and thread up at 1, down at 2, and up again at 3. Going back down at 1, continue in the same manner (Diagram I).

French Knots. Bring needle up at 1. Wrap floss once around needle and insert needle at 2, holding floss taut so that knot remains close to needle. Bring needle and floss down through fabric at 2, holding floss until it must be released (Diagram J).

Long Loose Stitch. Long loose stitches are represented in graphs and color codes by heavy black lines with dots at either end; dots indicate where needle is brought up and down. For very long stitches, couch floss at several points.

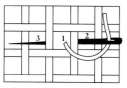

Diagram I

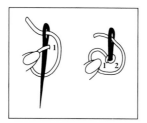

Diagram J

Special Thanks

The photographs in this book were taken at Attic Antiques, owned by Barbara Manning, and at the homes of Dru and Frank Carter, Peggy and Homer Dobbs, Rhonda and Bruce Dillard, Carla and Robert Ingram, Vicki and David Maxey, Jeanne and Mabry Rogers, Charlene and Bill Scharf, Barbara Stone, and Dean and Jerry Vandegrift.

Props were loaned by Country at Heart and Visions of Sugarplums, both of Birmingham, Alabama.

Special help was provided by Lisa G. Howard, owner of Stitch-n-Stuff, Birmingham, Alabama.

Alma Lynne Designs and Oxmoor House wish to thank each of them for their cooperation.

Suppliers

If you are unable to locate a particular fabric, your local needlework shop may order it from the following suppliers. You may also write to these suppliers for a list of needlework merchants near you.

Zweigart Fabrics—Zweigart/Joan Toggitt Ltd., Weston Canal Plaza, 2 Riverview Drive, Somerset, NJ 08873

Zweigart fabrics used:

Ivory 11-count Aida	Oatmeal 18-count Rustico Aida
Ash gray 14-count Aida	Mushroom 25-count Lugana
Ash rose 14-count Aida	Pewter 25-count Lugana
Celadon 14-count Aida	Wedgewood 25-count Lugana
Cream 14-count Gloria	Khaki 27-count Linda
Ivory 14-count Aida	Caramel 28-count Annabelle
Khaki 14-count Aida	Cream/tan 28-count Chalet
Parchment 14-count Yorkshire Aida	Dawn gray 28-count Jubilee
Bisque 18-count Davosa	Ivory 28-count Jubilee
Khaki 18-count Davosa	

Blueberry 14-count Aida, slate 14-count Aida, khaki 18-count Aida, tan 20-count Jobelan, white 20-count Jobelan, natural brown undyed 26-count linen, bluebell 30-count Shannon, natural brown undyed 30-count linen—Wichelt Imports, Inc., Rural Route 1, Stoddard, WI 54658

Ivory 21-count Glenshee Linen—Anne Powell Heirloom Stitchery, P.O. Box 3060, Stuart, FL 34995

Ivory 14-count Soft Touch, parchment 14-count Terry Towel, parchment 14-count Pot Holder—Charles Craft, P.O. Box 1049, Laurinburg, NC 28353

Cottage brown 24-count Heartland—Cross My Heart, Inc., 4725 Commercial Drive, Huntsville, AL 35816

1⅞"-wide ivory/burgundy 14-count Aida prefinished ribbon—Leisure Arts, Inc., P.O. Box 5595, Little Rock, AR 72215

Balger Products—Kreinik Manufacturing Company, Inc., 1708 Gihon Road, Parkersburg, WV 26101

144